THE WEALTH OF CITIES AND
THE POVERTY OF NATIONS

ECONOMIC TRANSFORMATIONS

Series Editors: Brett Christophers, Rebecca Lave, Jamie Peck, Marion Werner

Fundamental to the *Economic Transformations* series is the belief that "geography matters" in the diverse ways that economies work, for whom they work and to what ends. This series publishes books that evidence that conviction, creating a space for interdisciplinary contributions from political economists, economic geographers, feminists, political ecologists, economic sociologists, critical development theorists, economic anthropologists and their fellow travellers.

Published

Climate Finance: Taking a Position on Climate Futures
Gareth Bryant and Sophie Webber

The Doreen Massey Reader
Edited by Brett Christophers, Rebecca Lave, Jamie Peck and Marion Werner

Doreen Massey: Critical Dialogues
Edited by Marion Werner, Jamie Peck, Rebecca Lave and Brett Christophers

Exploring the Chinese Social Model: Beyond Market and State
Weidong Liu, Michael Dunford, Zhigao Liu and Zhenshan Yang

Farming as Financial Asset: Global Finance and the Making of Institutional Landscapes
Stefan Ouma

Labour Regimes and Global Production
Edited by Elena Baglioni, Liam Campling, Neil M. Coe and Adrian Smith

Market/Place: Exploring Spaces of Exchange
Edited by Christian Berndt, Jamie Peck and Norma M. Rantisi

The Wealth of Cities and the Poverty of Nations
Christof Parnreiter

THE WEALTH OF CITIES AND THE POVERTY OF NATIONS

CHRISTOF PARNREITER

agenda
publishing

In memory of my mother, who, well into her 90s,
still worried that the world had gone wrong

First published in 2024 by Agenda Publishing

Agenda Publishing Limited
PO Box 185
Newcastle upon Tyne
NE20 2DH

www.agendapub.com

ISBN 978-1-78821-558-9 (hardcover)
ISBN 978-1-78821-559-6 (paperback)

British Library Cataloguing-in-Publication Data
A catalogue record for this book is available from the British Library

Typeset in Warnock by Patty Rennie

Printed and bound in the UK by CPI Group (UK) Ltd, Croydon, CR0 4YY

CONTENTS

PREFACE

This is a book about the role of cities in the production of uneven development, a topic with which I have been preoccupied since I was an undergraduate, and that I have approached from different angles since then. Interested in understanding the mechanisms and geographies of exploitation of what was then still called the "Third World", I plunged into world-systems analysis (Wallerstein 1974a, 1983), which we were assigned as course reading. The course lecturer also sparked my interest in cities, especially through Braudel-influenced lectures on the cities of northern Italy. I am grateful to Peter Feldbauer for introducing me to a city-centred view of capitalism and its uneven development, and for making me read the emerging literature on peripheral urbanization. One of these books was Michael Timberlake's (1985) *Urbanization in the World Economy*, and Bryan Roberts' sympathetic but critical review became the guide – or mandate – for my own research interests. To most of the contributions to the Timberlake book, Roberts levels the criticism that "[r]elationships of inequality are taken as given, but the mechanisms by which power is exercised and reproduced are not fully examined ... There is not enough emphasis ... on *how cities and the classes within them achieve control over other regions*" (1986: 459; emphasis in original). After almost 40 years since Roberts urged a comprehensive treatment of the question of "how cities and the classes within them achieve control over other regions", our knowledge of this is still rudimentary. But worse still, the question has been relegated to the background in both urban studies and in analyses of uneven development, which is why I was prompted to write this book.

To address the challenge of how "cities" and "classes within them" could be brought together in the analysis of the mechanisms of uneven development, I found current debates about the specialness of cities, conducted in different disciplines (e.g. economic geography, regional economics, urban sociology) and across theoretical positions very instructive. They have a common denominator: cities are extraordinary (Taylor 2013) because they have certain properties that are "intrinsically urban in character" (Scott & Storper 2015: 9) and that enable the actors within cities to be more innovative and productive than people elsewhere. Agglomeration, the embeddedness in inter-city networks and the massiveness of the built environment are the properties underlying the "genius of cities" (Storper 2013), and allows them to become the "mothers of economic development", as Jane Jacobs (1997), an urban theorist, activist and patroness of the unconditional belief in cities' extraordinariness, summarizes a broad consensus in urban research. Seeing capitalism in such a way, through the lens of cities and to explain its growth dynamics by cities' properties, is an endeavour that Peter Taylor (2013) called a city-centred narrative, and which I call a "citified" perspective.

This book builds on the consensus that cities are a central analytical category for understanding the economy because their properties enhance the capacity of the actors within them to pursue their interests. However, I also seek to break with an important element of the current consensus. Today's discourse on cities is rife with unbridled positivity, not least as the consummate drivers of economic growth and social development. Not everyone would put it as boldly as US economist Edward Glaeser (2011), but in essence his book title captures the *zeitgeist* well: *Triumph of the City: How Our Greatest Invention Makes Us Richer, Smarter, Greener, Healthier, and Happier*. Across the political and social-scientific spectrum, the city is praised for its innovative potential and efficiency, whereas critical tones are only heard insofar as problems in cities (such as poverty, housing shortage, segregation, etc.) are addressed. What does not exist, however, is a *citified* understanding of uneven development, in the sense that Bryan Roberts calls for. In urban studies, cities have been divorced from the study of the asymmetrical relationships that constitute the capitalist division of labour, with the result that their generative power has become exclusively associated with growth, but not with exploitation, as if, in capitalism, one is not causally linked to the other. In debates on uneven development, in turn, such as those of the various strands of global commodity chain research, the city does not appear at all as an analytical category (and is largely neglected even as a location for economic activities)

With this book, I want to bring dissonance into this discourse of "positive thinking" about cities. Although I do not question cities' extraordinary vitality and ability to spark economic, social and political dynamics, I object to the one-sided representation of the workings of this urban potential: I posit that they are not only positive, do not exclusively bring forth the "good" (growth, development), but that they also generate the "bad" (exploitation, oppression). Doubting whether cities make *all of us* "richer, smarter, greener, healthier, and happier", irrespective of social, geographical and historical contexts, I argue that the genius of cities is Janus-faced, that is, acting in opposite ways. My intention is to launch a citified analysis of uneven development, to make the city an analytical category for the understanding of how it is produced and sustained. Examining the organization and functioning of uneven development through the lens of cities should reveal the extent to which "elites depend on urban contexts for capital accumulation" (van Heur & Bassens 2019: 591), that is, for the organization of exploitation, which is, after all, the basis of capitalist accumulation.

This idea, of course, is far from new. When I say that I want to bring dissonance into the debate about the nature of cities, it would be more accurate to say that I want to recall the dissonant voices that have always existed but were louder in the past and to bring a citified analysis of uneven development back to the top of the agenda. Partly through rather isolated thoughts, partly in theoretically adept debates, partly in empirically rich descriptions, the ambivalent role cities play in capitalism has been examined critically time and again since the emergence of economics as a discipline. The aim of this book is to retrieve some of these accounts, but not to discuss them comprehensively. Nor will I be able to address the contradictions that exist between the authors cited in the overall thrust of their arguments. But that is not my concern either. Developing a specific storyline by drawing on scholars from many fields, and from different eras, will certainly not do justice to all the thoughts developed by them. What I do claim, however, is to do justice to their respective specific contributions to a specific topic, with the aim of making them fruitful for contemporary debates on the nature of cities.

The book essentially speaks to two different scholarly audiences. It is an invitation to those interested in the city to learn about a view that is less biased towards growth, less developmentalist. This does not mean it provides a balanced understanding of the city, in the sense of everything having its own pros and cons. Nor is it my intention to draw a dystopian picture of cities. I am convinced of the economic power of cities as well as of their potential to promote social mobility and democratization. What I am striving for is, however, an understanding of cities' role in the economy and society that does justice to the contradictions of capitalism, an assessment which "acknowledge[s] and understand[s] the close relationship between dark and bright sides *and what analysis of one brings to the other*" (Phelps *et al.* 2018: 237; emphasis added). For me, this call means using what we have learned from urban research about the exceptionality of cities to develop a citified understanding of uneven development. Accordingly, the book is also an invitation to all those interested in uneven development. In the literatures gathered under this umbrella, geographical imagination has evolved, under the influence of the various strands of global commodity chain research, from a state-centred perspective that dominated modernization theoretical thinking to an emphasis on networks. Interestingly, however, with the exception of some contributions to the global city debate, little attention has been paid to the nodes of these networks – cities. This is a pity, because an examination of the actors who organize exploitation, and their geographies, could benefit enormously from the insights that urban studies has produced about the nature and functioning of cities.

Combining these insights with knowledge created in past decades about the role of cities in capitalist exploitation and uneven development, I hope that this book will be of practical value for readers in the sense that it can provide suggestions for fruitfully addressing how "cities and the classes within them achieve control over other regions". Regarding my hope that this book will be of practical value, I have one more point concerning the language. I have been encouraged by the publisher and series editors to speak to a wider audience, both in the sense of overcoming disciplinary boundaries and of reaching not just established researchers, but also students and even readers beyond the academic community. With these readers in mind, and not just academic colleagues, the writing style is perhaps a little more essayistic than is usually the case in scientific publications, and even a little provocative in places. But still, I have tried to reflect and engage with academic debates and to develop an argument. I do hope that readers will find this interesting and worthwhile.

Finally, I would like to thank some people who helped me to develop and sharpen my thoughts, to correct mistakes and to broaden views. I have already mentioned Peter Feldbauer. David Bassens, Christin Bernhold, Ben Deruder, Stefan Krätke, Jürgen Oßenbrügge, Kunibert Raffer, Peter Taylor and Michiel van Meeteren have been in discussion with me over the years as I worked on the paper (Parnreiter 2022) of which this book is, in a sense, the adult form. I am very grateful to the editors of Agenda's Economic Transformations series, Brett Christophers, Rebecca Lave, Jamie Peck and Marion Werner, for inviting and encouraging me to write this book. I thank the three anonymous reviewers for their challenging suggestions, but even more for the empathy for the overall project in which these were presented. Alison Howson at Agenda was great to work with, and special thanks for discussing individual terms (such as "citified") with me. Christin Bernhold, Jürgen Ossenbrügge, Bryan Roberts, Michiel van Meeteren and Marion Werner read the draft manuscript and helped with critical advice, but also faith in the overall argument. Klara Kolhoff has provided me with research on specific questions, and with technical matters, as did Katharina Vöhler.

My biggest thanks go to Leon and Magdalena, for all the conversations, meals together, travels and soccer matches.

CHAPTER 1

INTRODUCTION

"Cities are at the frontier of development; they are where people go to chase their dreams of a better life for themselves and their families", said Juergen Voegele, the World Bank's Vice President for Sustainable Development, when presenting the bank's analysis *Pancakes to Pyramids: City Form for Sustainable Growth* (World Bank 2021; Lall *et al.* 2021). This is one of many statements that demonstrate how, in the last two decades, the idea that "the city has triumphed" (Glaeser 2011), has become the credo of most of urban studies, the publications of international organizations and business consult-ancies. Gone are the days of the "'hate literature' on cities" (Taylor 2004: 3) that produced urban dystopias such as *Planet of Slums*, in which Mike Davis (2006) portrays the big cities of the Global South as an evil, as an obstacle to rather than as a means of development. Today, the notion that cities, both in the North and South, boost innovation, productivity and efficiency, and that they are therefore engines of economic growth and social development is a given. The acknowledgement of cities' extraordinariness (cf. Taylor 2013), of urbanization's "efficiency-generating qualities via agglomeration" (Scott & Storper 2015: 4), of cities "as innovation machine[s]" (Florida *et al.* 2017) and "mothers of economic development" (Jacobs 1997), and of the "urban ability to create collaborative brilliance" (Glaeser 2011: 8) are prevalent. Not even postcolonial scholars, critical of the universalization of ideas origin-ating in the Global North (e.g. Robinson 2006), have challenged the notion of the "almost universal positive association" (Brockerhoff & Brennan 1998: 82) between urbanization and economic development. It is not surprising, then, that Andrew Kirby (2012: 3) concludes from his bibliometric analysis of social science journals that the "study of cities is in many ways a study of human development". "Development" is one of the words most frequently associated in urban research with the words "urban", "city" or "cities" (in 2010). Accordingly, the economic power of cities has become something of an *idée fixe* among development agencies (e.g. World Bank 2009a; World Bank Institute 2010) and consulting firms (e.g. Dobbs *et al.* 2011).

And indeed, a quick look at the geographies of economic production and productivity (output per unit of input, such as labour time or capital) confirms these assessments. In the early 2000s, 80 per cent of global GDP already stemmed from cities alone, three quarters of which was being produced in only 600 cities. In 2018, 15 per cent of total world production originated from people's work in just 17 cities, with New York, Tokyo, Los Angeles, Paris and Seoul leading the way (Euromonitor International 2019; World Bank 2013; Dobbs *et al.* 2011). In OECD countries, capital cities contribute on average more than 26 per cent to the GDP of their respective countries – a trend that is increasing (OECD 2018). Moreover, if one compares the contribution of cities to GDP with their share of the population (at the national, regional or global level), one finds that people in cities are more productive than elsewhere. For example, the share of the 20 largest urban economies of total world production is almost five times greater than their corresponding share in total population, with US cities such as Chicago, New York and Los Angeles standing out for their particularly high productivity (see Figure 1.1).

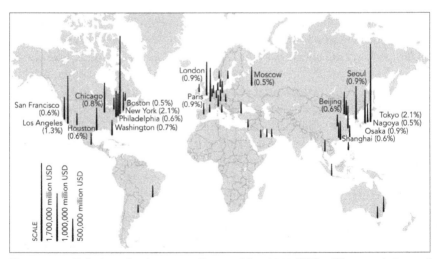

Figure 1.1 Global production according to cities, 2018 (US$ millions and share of world gross value added)
Source: Own presentation. Data: Euromonitor International 2019.

We can agree, then, with the World Bank (2021) – cities are indeed "the frontier of development". Cities and the networks they form on the national, regional and global scales are not just a result or expression of development, they constitute an essential input in themselves. The wealth of nations, which preoccupies economists, does not come from nations, but from their *cities* (cf. Jacobs 1985).

While I fully agree with these ideas, there is nevertheless a problem with "the city is the solution" discourse. This problem is *not* that it portrays cities as places of economic dynamism and possible (indeed, likely) social mobility. The problem is that this notion is built on two theoretical assumptions about the relationship between cities and development that are highly questionable. First, today's prevailing view is based on a conception of development – and the poverty it is supposed to overcome – which is naïve at best, i.e. lacking in critical analysis and reasoning (at worst, this view can be accused of deceptive intent, of deliberately misleading about the causes of poverty). There is a bias towards developmentalism that is as strong as it was in the heyday of modernization theory in the 1950s and 1960s.[1] Poverty is seen as a society's original state, which is characterized by the absence of anything that would allow for development: division of labour and markets, entrepreneurial spirit, industrialization, foreign trade, rational decision-making, modern attitudes, and so on. Central to the theme of this book is that in modernization theory, urbanization is one of the principal changes that any society has to undergo if it wishes to develop, that is, to become prosperous. Consequently, and this is the second basic theoretical assumption I object to, the prevailing view of the relationship between cities and development is utterly one-sided, biased toward the "bright side", toward the positive effects that come from cities. However, their possible "dark sides", the idea that cities may have something to do not only with overcoming poverty but also with creating it and profiting from it, is hardly found in today's debates, not in academia, and certainly not among international organizations and business consultancies.

---

1. By "developmentalism" an understanding of economic and social development is meant which assumes that societies develop in a linear movement from traditional to modern, following the pattern of Western countries. The foundation for this thinking has been provided by modernization theory, a set of concepts that sought to explain modernization as processes of economic and social development based on the model of Western countries. Modernization was cast as an evolutionary route in which any society that wanted to advance had to pass through certain stages of development. Crucially, a country's level of development is seen as being caused mainly by endogenous factors rather than by economic or political relations at a regional or global scale. Modernization theory also sought to provide policies in order to support such development.

Of course, these two conceptual problems are interrelated. The unquestioning belief in the brilliance of cities arises from a harmonious notion of capitalism, in which poverty is "just there", as a spontaneous state of deficiency, and not as the result of political-economic processes, of an intentional "taking away", of exploitation and subsequent pauperization. (I quite generally refer to exploitation as the appropriation of the fruits of other people's labour). Statements from prevalent voices in the current debate on urban theory make clear the developmentalist foundation of the "brilliance of cities" discourse. The great theorist and urban activist Jane Jacobs (1970: 120f.) says, for example – and this sentence is to a certain extent the leitmotif of her work – that "[t]o seek 'causes' of poverty . . . is to enter an intellectual dead end because poverty has no causes. Only prosperity has causes". For her, the great admirer of the dynamism of cities, these causes are cities (and only cities). A similar developmentalist approach to cities without any restriction is also put forward by Michael Storper, one of today's most influential economic and urban geographers. His central contributions to the debate about "The Nature of Cities" (Scott & Storper 2015; see also Storper 2010, 2013; Storper & Scott 2016) do not mention exploitation at all, and uneven development only as a byproduct (albeit a necessary one) of the urbanization of the economy, which unavoidably creates differences between places with more productive economic activities and places with fewer and less productive activities: "Cities are key . . . to greater wealth creation, but they involve equity or distributional effects: higher average incomes in some places than others, and possibly higher inequality within them" (Storper 2013: 49).

I take issue with the theoretical axioms that undergird this one-sided belief in progress brought about by cities by arguing that we need to elaborate a more comprehensive understanding of the connection between cities and development. And that includes a more comprehensive understanding of "development". Capitalism is not only about growth and wealth creation, but also about – and causally connected with – exploitation and impoverishment. Development, thus, is polarizing, creating both winners and losers. Accordingly, if we want to fully understand the role of cities in capitalism, we must not only refer to the bright side. Because capitalist growth – namely, accumulation – is inherently related to the production and appropriation of surplus value, the city must have something to do with both the wealth of nations as well as with their misery, with development and with exploitation. A core idea of the book, then, is that the genius of cities, of which Storper (2013) speaks quite appropriately, is Janus-faced, acting in opposite ways. Cities are not only nodes in global networks of production, but also in "poverty chains" (Selwyn 2019). Hence the title of this book: *The Wealth of*

Cities and the Poverty of Nations. If Jane Jacobs turned Adam Smith's *Inquiry into the Nature and Causes of the Wealth of Nations* (1776) into an inquiry into "Cities" *and the Wealth of Nations* (1985) in order to emphasize the generative power of cities, my book title stresses the ambiguity of this generative power.

With this in mind my understanding of "node" follows Peter Taylor (2013: 219), who conceptualizes cities' nodality as being *"proactive"*, i.e. as taking actions that are intended to cause changes, rather than just reflecting them. This implies assuming a certain spatial effectiveness – space is not a mere stage or container for social processes, but their part (which, however, must not be equated with spatial determinism – cities do not act themselves, but they provide a specific setting which offers incentives for action; see Chapter 3). Such spatial effectiveness is taken for granted by all who conceptualize cities as drivers of economic development. Across disciplines and theoretical positions, cities' economic proactiviness is consensual, as evidenced for example by the fact that it is uncontroversial that cities generate positive economic externalities. These are benefits that result from a "situation" and accrue to third parties, even if these are not directly involved in the "situation" itself. Agglomeration economies are certainly the most important externalities attributed to the "urban condition", but externalities also arise from inter-city networks and the massiveness of the built environment (see Chapter 3). Interestingly, however, it goes largely unnoticed that it is not particularly plausible that the spatial effectiveness should work only in one direction, that it engenders the "good" innovation only, which is the basis for growth and development. The "bad" innovations, the ever new means to exploit and oppress people, seem to come from nowhere. However, if in capitalism networks of production are at the same time networks of exploitation, and if we ascribe to cities a proactive role in the former, then it follows that this proactivity must also refer to the latter, to exploitation and uneven development.

This claim presupposes a specific understanding of uneven development, namely one in which poverty is neither "just there", as an initial condition (as in Jane Jacobs), nor that uneven development occurs somehow as a byproduct of development (as in Michael Storper) (for more details, see Chapter 2). Rather, I think of uneven development as the result of exploitation, which is intentionally organized by capitalist actors and in two distinct but interrelated forms and geographies. Capitalism, writes Immanuel Wallerstein (1974a: 401), founder of world-systems analysis, "involves not only appropriation of the surplus-value by an owner from a laborer, but an appropriation of surplus of the whole world-economy by core areas". These two dimensions of exploitation are not merely juxtaposed (additive, as it were), but they mutually reinforce each other – surpluses drained from peripheries, fed by the exploitation of labour there, nourish and accelerate accumulation processes in the cores of the capitalist world-system, which in turn enables capitalists there to exploit (both locally and across space) on extended stages (Wallerstein 1983).

The appropriation of surplus of the whole world-economy by core areas – or, in other words, geographical transfers of value or surplus[2] – requires agency (Hadjimichalis 1984), it is organized and controlled by certain actors, through specific practices and mechanisms[3] (such as unequal exchange and profit repatriation), and from specific places. This is how cities come into play. I propose that they are causally linked to uneven development because they are the places from where value or surplus transfers are planned, managed and controlled. This is not only true in the topographical sense, that is, as a description: New York as a specific location from where capitalist actors produce uneven development. Rather, cities are key places for value or surplus transfers in an analytical sense. Uneven development is organized and controlled from cities, because cities' inherent properties empower city-based actors in ways that allow them to shape the global economy as they see fit and in their best interests. In this sense, uneven development is produced not only in, but *through* cities. This is my understanding of cities as proactive nodes: they are engines of growth, yes, but *as such*, they also provide the environment in which can be forged what

---

2. Wallerstein does not use the term "surplus value" as strictly and well-defined as classical Marxists, for whom *Mehrwert* is the objectification of unpaid labour time of a *wage* worker. Wallerstein speaks of "surplus" and "surplus value" alternately, and he associates the latter not only with unpaid labour time of wage workers, but also with rent squeezed out of direct rural producers, the overseas plantations economy, which could be based on slavery, share-cropping or wage labour, and with the putting-out system and its formally independent producers. Overall, in world-systems analysis, "surplus" or "surplus value" refer to "profit" – the difference between costs and revenue, regardless of the specific relations of production in which exploited workers find themselves. Accordingly, when Wallerstein (1974a: 401) refers to the "appropriation of the surplus-value by an owner from a laborer", merchants could just as well be meant by "owners" as industrialists, while "laborer" could refer to wage workers as well as small farmers or merchants and slaves. I refrain here from a more detailed discussion of "value" and "surplus" to avoid what Harvey has called "an accounting nightmare (*which, in my view, is insoluble*)" (2013: 92; emphasis added). This analysis would require wrestling with the thorny issues of Marx's law of value and the "transformation problem", which is not possible within the scope of this book.

3. By a mechanism I mean social processes that become causally effective because of their regularity.

the French historian Fernand Braudel (1984: 35) has called, the "weapons of domination".

Building on this reasoning of Braudel, this book is a plea to take the city as an analytical category in reflections about uneven development, as an *explanans* (sentences presented as explanations of a phenomenon) that helps us to understand how uneven development is produced and maintained. I see cities as bases of resources, material and intangible ones, which are mobilized by city-based capitalist actors in order to exercise economic power, to gain control over people, in the same city or far away (for the concept of power, see Allen 2003).

What are these resources? What is the specificity of the urban environment, to which Braudel refers to? Allan Scott (2017: 16) claims that every city has "certain intrinsic and generalizable features . . . [which] distinguish specifically urban phenomena from the rest of society". There is broad agreement across disciplines that the most elementary of these characteristics is agglomeration, the clustering of social actors, relations and processes in relatively confined spaces, resulting in a specific density and diversity. For Storper (2013: 9) agglomeration is the basis of what he calls the "particular 'genius'" of cities. Cities are exceptional (to paraphrase Taylor [2013]) because their density and diversity create a "behavioral context in which different elements of know-how come together . . . [in which] interaction takes a specific form . . . [because of the] many overlapping worlds of face-to-face contact, giving them a 'buzz'" (Storper 2013: 9–10). I embrace Storper's notion of the genius of cities, but with two important modifications. First, I add two more elements to agglomeration as one of its foundations, namely cities' embeddedness in networks that connect them to other cities, from the immediate hinterland to the ends of the world (this aspect has been emphasized in particular by Jane Jacobs [1970], Allen Pred [1977] and Peter Taylor [2004]); and the massiveness of the physical infrastructure, the built environment (which David Harvey [e.g. 1985] has repeatedly pointed out). Like agglomeration, both are "intrinsic and generalizable features" of cities.

The second modification I make to Storper's concept of the genius of cities concerns its assessment. Whereas Storper (2013) positively connotes the genius of cities throughout, I claim that it is Janus-faced, that is, looking or acting in opposite or contrasting ways. My central argument is that the same characteristics of cities – agglomeration, embeddedness into inter-city networks, and a massive built environment – which make them so extraordinarily proficient at producing the "good" innovations, provide fertile ground for the development of the "bad" ones too. Of course, what is a positive and what is a negative development is a philosophical question and implies a

7

normative appreciation. Following Erich Fromm, psychoanalyst and philosopher associated with the Frankfurt School of critical theory, I would say that "good" innovations are those that serve the unfolding of people's potential, with "people" referring to "the many" rather than the "the few" (a distinction popularized by the Occupy Wall Street movement in 2011). This includes the satisfaction of material and social needs, and insofar a certain degree of prosperity, but also freedom, self-determination and a community. "Bad" innovation brings about the opposite, namely developments that promote the enrichment of a few at the expense of the many (I discuss two examples of this, namely the making of super-profits through super-exploitation and through the establishment of monopolies, in Chapter 5).

The point being that while I agree with the literature that cities foster auspicious developments, because their "specific supply architecture" (Storper 2013: 9) drives learning, improving and inventing, I contend that they do the same for undesirable and bad developments. If Bas van Heur and David Bassens (2019: 591) contend that "elites depend on urban contexts for capital accumulation, consumption and leisure, and housing", then I argue that this applies to *all dimensions* of accumulation, and not only to growth, but also to exploitation and polarization. Urban elites depend on urban contexts to develop the means to exploit others as efficiently as possible. Cities are motors of development, and at the same time and for the same reasons, they are nodes from where its unevenness is organized. They provide the fertile ground on which urban elites have developed since the emergence of capitalism (and likely even earlier) the means with which they have syphoned off wealth from other localities and regions. In our attempts to understand capitalism, Braudel says, "we shall be particularly concerned" with cities and the networks they form, because "these connections, meeting-points and multiple links . . . *reveal the way in which a dominant economy can exploit subordinate economies*" (1984: 248; emphasis added).

It is not that cities' dark sides are not acknowledged in the literature – urban poverty, segregation or exclusion, to name but a few, are the subjects of many studies. Yet, it is one thing to examine problems *in* cities, and another to put cities centre stage as a fundamental analytical category for analysing how the "poverty of nations" is created. So, it is not enough to understand the relationship between wealth creation and poverty generation, but we should do so from a *citified* perspective, that is, seen through the lens of cities. This implies conceptualizing cities as *proactive* nodes in the asymmetric connectivities of divisions of labour at various scales through which exploitation across space is organized.

The book is structured as follows: in the next chapter, I begin by clarifying a term central to my argument, namely what I mean by "uneven development" (see Chapter 2). Following on from this, the third chapter is devoted to laying out the urban theoretical foundations of the book. I begin with defining what a city is to me, to then discuss the genius of cities and the externalities from which it arises, namely agglomeration, inter-city networks and the built environment. In addition, I shall assess the relationship between structure and agency, and what this means for a citified analysis of uneven development. In Chapter 4, I present literature that has inspired my critical reasoning about cities and that has led me to think that their genius is Janus-faced: debates about the role of cities in the transition from feudalism to capitalism in Europe; thoughts of Adam Smith and Karl Marx on the uneven relationships between town and country; Fernand Braudel's analysis of the rise of capitalism as being city-driven; and critical analysis of the role of (capital) cities in the "development of underdevelopment" in Latin America, as André Gunder Frank's (1969) brilliant formulation puts it. Despite significant differences among these scholars (differences of theoretical nature, the time in and about which they wrote, and their respective geographical focus), they all understand the role of the city in capitalist development as proactive, even "aggressive" (cf. Baudel 1984: 94) in *two* respects: as entrepreneurial, tearing down old barriers to pave the way for new worlds, and as a desire and practice to dominate and exploit others. The chapter seeks to recover knowledge that is in danger of being lost, in order to make it fruitful for contemporary thinking about the connection between cities and development. Chapter 5 uses the findings of these literatures to outline how current research on the role of cities in relations of exploitation might proceed, using two examples, namely lawyers specializing in labour law on the side of corporations, enabling them to super-exploit workers in the peripheries, and in intellectual property, establishing monopolies for their clients. Both undoubtedly play an important role in the production of uneven development. In the final chapter I use the citified analysis that I have deployed here for a further development of world-systems analysis, in order to fulfill a request made by Peter Taylor some 20 years ago, namely "[c]asting cities into a starring role in a world-systems analysis" (2003: 131).

CHAPTER 2

UNEVEN DEVELOPMENT

I begin my project of developing a citified analysis of uneven development by first explaining what I mean by it. Uneven development generally refers to the fact that the economy grows more in some places than in others. Economic performance varies across space, at different levels, from the urban to the global scale, and wealth therefore becomes geographically unequally distributed. Whereas understanding uneven development in terms of economic inequalities across space is likely to be consensual across disciplines and theoretical currents, views as to how this inequality came about differ widely. Roughly speaking, two approaches can be distinguished.

The "differentiated growth model" explains uneven development primarily as a process of spatially bound self-expansion of capital, which is why Costis Hadjimichalis (1984) refers to this view as the "autonomous or semi-autonomous development thesis". The gist of this argument is that economic growth dynamics are geographically variegated, because they result from endogenous and therefore clearly localizable factors such as natural endowments or agglomeration economies. Because these factors are inherent to certain places but not others, growth "naturally" varies across space and inequality is the unavoidable result. Whereas economic relationships (e.g. investment, trade, migration) between the respective spatial units of analysis – mostly thought of as states, sometimes as regions or cities – are not negated by proponents of the "differentiated growth model", they do not have a formative role in the emergence of inequality. The core idea of this approach to uneven development is therefore *non-relational*: states, regions or cities develop differently, but they do so due to endogenous conditions and hence by and large independently and detached from each other. Economic expansion in one place is consequently unrelated to stagnation or even contraction in another. Uneven development occurs because the more productive economies are pulling away, leaving the slower or stagnating nations, regions and cities behind. Because growth tends to beget new growth, uneven development proceeds in a self-reinforcing spiral, and economic and social asymmetries deepen over time. However, in this model, it is also conceivable that the endogenous growth factors lose strength, i.e. that former frontrunners stagnate or fall behind (for different versions of the "differentiated growth" model, see Jacobs 1970 and Storper 2013; for its policy significance, see, e.g., World Bank 2009a).

The emphasis on endogenous factors being responsible for growth and accordingly the downplaying of (asymmetric) economic relationships across space for the occurrence of uneven development, has an important implication: in the differentiated growth model, uneven development is not the result of intentional actions, but a by-product of "normal" development. Urbanization creates, says Storper (2013: 4), "a form of extreme unevenness: it packs people, firms, information, and wealth into small territories", with the consequence that "[c]onvergence is in many ways an averaging illusion". I have, however, already indicated that I do not share assessments that conceive of uneven development in such a way. In contrast, I have argued that uneven development is the result of deliberate action, namely exploitation. Such an understanding is a political-economic one.

Political economy is the study of how a society organizes its economy, that is, how production, exchange and consumption are realized and regulated. This organizing of the economy is always political in the sense that it is neither a given nor without alternatives. It always results from choices made in a society, and therefore from how – and how successful – certain actors or social groups can pursue their objectives and assert their interests (and who is among the losers in this process, and why). These interests involve a wide range of topics: from issues of ownership (who owns the means of production?) to what is produced, by whom, under which conditions, and where (this includes, for example, the geography of commodity chains, whether and how easily monopolies are allowed to exist, or labour legislation); to the question of how to distribute what has been produced and how to use the surplus generated (who gets which slices of the pie?); and what the causes of recurrent crises are, possible ways of overcoming them, and who bears the costs. All these questions imply issues of inequality, for which reason political economy in general is about questions of power. Marxist political economy, however, is distinguished by its explicit critique of these asymmetric power relations: Marx's subtitle to *Capital, A Critique of Political Economy* corresponds to a radical (in the sense of fundamental and relentless) analysis of the social conditions for the endless accumulation of capital and its consequences (namely exploitation and polarization), with the goal not only to reveal the secrets of capitalists' *"Plusmacherei"* (profit-making; Marx [1890] 1962), but to overcome it.

Back to conceptualizations of uneven development. The "differentiated growth model" is contrasted with what Eric Sheppard (2016: 158) calls "connectivity-based explanations". These underscore the importance that "asymmetric connectivities . . . [and the] deleterious socio-spatial positionalities" (*ibid.*) of people and regions in divisions of labour at various scales have for uneven development. While such relational approaches do consider localized (and hence spatially differentiated) elements for economic development (such as spatially confined agglomeration economies or accumulation dynamics) as drivers of geographical unevenness, they emphasize that there is more about uneven development than differentiated growth. Wealth transfers across space in form of value or surplus transfers are identified as one of its most important, perhaps even the most important mechanism, because they give rise to and nourish geographically differentiated growth dynamics. In this understanding, uneven development is a relational process whereby the development in one place is achieved at least in part through the exploitation of people in another place, where growth is accordingly slowed down or made impossible altogether. In this respect, connectivity-based explanations of uneven development are more in line with the idea of political-economic analysis that the organization of the economy (including its unevenness) has to be explained than the differentiated growth model and its focus on the spatially bound self-expansion of capital.

Moreover, connectivity-based explanations of uneven development take seriously the credo of critical human geography that space matters for the ways a society organizes the economy (e.g. Harvey [1982] 2006; Massey [1984] 1995; Soja 1989). They therefore represent a *spatialized* political-economic analysis in which "the economy" and "geography" are not treated as separate worlds or in a hierarchy, first production and then its geography. Nor is it adequate for a spatialized political-economic analysis to consider space in a banal manner that presumes it is sufficient to locate economic activities in specific geographical containers (as, for example, when speaking of automobile production in China, financial industries in London, etc.). Rather, as Doreen Massey ([1984] 1995: 56) urges us, "'[g]eography' should be part of the specification from the beginning". Accordingly, spatializing political-economic analysis entails the challenge of showing that the relations of production[4] are not only "in space", but rather *structured spatially*, and that

---

4. The relations of production include all relationships that people enter into in the processes of production, circulation and consumption. They account for the hierarchization of the division of labour and the social stratification of a society (e.g. into classes).

this geographical organization impacts on their nature. Consequently, the task of a spatialized political-economic analysis is to reveal that the ways in which a society organizes production and exchange geographically shapes the generation and distribution of the wealth produced. It draws attention to the modes of how certain actors produce economic landscapes by developing economic activities and relationships *through* (rather than in) these geographies, and how they thereby structure the economy and the distribution of wealth in their favour.

Massey's ([1984] 1995) interpretation of the division of labour as the spatialization of power relations was groundbreaking for such a relational understanding of uneven development. Starting from the observation (which now sounds like a commonplace, thanks, among other things, to the rethinking that Massey has initiated) that the social relations of production necessarily develop spatially because the economy unfolds within real geographies and not on a pinhead as mainstream economists would have us believe, and arguing that space matters for any dimension of human life, she claims that the specific geography given to a division of labour by investment (and disinvestment) decisions of companies matters for its social dynamics. And more specifically she points out that the asymmetric relationships of dominance–subordination, exploitation and inequality that sustain capitalist accumulation are produced and reproduced through concrete spatial arrangements. Intensified exploitation, for example by depressing wages, is facilitated, if not made possible, by the relocation of industrial jobs to peripheral areas (whether domestically or on a global scale). Accordingly, the economic landscapes we live in, the specific geography that makes us speak of industrial regions, low-wage countries or financial centres, result from "unequal relationships", from "the stretching out over space of the relations of economic ownership and of possession" (Massey 2004: 87). Massey's contribution to understanding uneven development, then, is not only to have imposed a relational, connectivity-based understanding in economic geography, but also to have shown that the geographies of these connections (i.e., the spatial patterns of the division of labour) matter greatly. Massey made us think about the geographical distribution of activities, jobs, functions, etc., not in technical but in qualitative terms, interpreting them as emerging from a purposeful and asymmetric organization of the social relations of production across space.

Asymmetric relations between regions and countries are also key to explaining uneven development in theories of unequal exchange and in dependency theory (Prebisch 1950; Singer 1950; Baran [1957] 1973; Baran & Sweezy 1966; Frank 1969; Emmanuel 1972; Marini 1973; Amin 1976). Beginning in the 1950s, these approaches began to confront the then hegemonic modernization theory and its reasoning that in capitalism development (ultimately understood as higher prosperity) would be possible for *all* countries, if they only take the right political and economic measures and follow the path of "the West" (hence the term "developing countries"). Moreover, unequal exchange and dependency theory scholars have also distinguished themselves (albeit to varying degrees) from traditional Marxist analysis by paying attention not only to the sphere of production, in which capitalists exploit wage workers, but also to the circulation sphere, in which rich (or core) countries exploit poor (or peripheral) countries.[5] Paul Baran ([1957] 1973: 311), for example, claimed that the normal course of capitalism is to cause ever more divergence in economic development paths of countries and regions instead of convergence, because "underdeveloped" and "advanced" countries were linked to each other through "transfers of surplus" that represented a "significant drain on capital accumulation" for the countries from which the "profits" were withdrawn. This is, of course, a very different explanation for the persistence of divergent development paths than the one given by Storper (2013: 60) for his claim that "[c]onvergence is . . . an averaging illusion". Similarly to Baran, dependency theorist Frank (1967: 9) insists that capitalism is a polarizing system, with the basic mechanism of the polarization being that "the metropolis expropriates economic surplus from its satellites and appropriates it for its own economic development. The satellites remain underdeveloped for lack of access to their own surplus". Emmanuel (1972) and Amin (1976), on the other hand, in their theories of unequal exchange, focused on wage differentials between core and peripheral countries. In the latter, they argued, wages are significantly lower, not because labour productivity is lower, but because they are politically depressed to allow capitalists to make extra profits (I shall return to this issue in Chapter 5). If these countries enter into trade relations with core countries, the exchange between them becomes unequal, because amounts of labour are traded that are equally productive (i.e. producing the same amount of goods in a certain unit of time), but are renummerated differently. "[W]henever labor of the same productivity is rewarded at a lower rate", says Amin (1976: 149), exchange between countries is unequal.

With such theoretical assessments of underdevelopment, as it was then called, the spatial antagonisms between countries and regions were placed on an equal footing with the social ones between capitalists and workers. In

---

5. Critics object that this shift in focus distracts from the fact that surplus value is created and appropriated only in production.

world-systems analysis,[6] which in the 1970s became arguably the most influ-ential critique of capitalism alongside classical Marxism, the geographical dimension of analysis acquired its clearest expression. Strongly building on Baran, dependency theory and the notion of unequal exchange, Immanuel Wallerstein (1974a) expounded in the "founding manifesto" of world-systems analysis that the exploitative relations which are constitutive of capitalism consist of two dimensions and two geographies, namely asymmetries between capitalists and labourers, and between core and peripheral areas of the world economy. Whereas the first form of exploitation, the uneven relations between owners and labourers, unfolds primarily (but not exclu-sively) at the local or national level, the appropriation of surplus by core areas necessarily evolves trans-locally, across space. According to world-systems analysis, the vertical (owner–labourer) and horizontal (core–periphery) dimensions of exploitation are inseparable in capitalism. Asymmetric relations between classes and between regions are thus treated as equally weighted – the relations of exploitation that underlie capitalist accumula-tion are organized on various levels, from local to global. "The fact is", writes Wallerstein, "that historical capitalism has been up to now a system of very differential rewards, *in both class and geographic terms*" (1991: 108; emphasis added). The latter can be seen as so elemental to capitalism that they can even be considered synonymous with its history (Cope 2019).

Given Wallerstein's elaboration on capitalism's geographical antago-nisms, it is not surprising that he pays close attention to the spatial strategies on which its main actors have relied on from the beginning to assert their interests. To ensure the endless accumulation of capital and its simultaneous concentration in the hands of a few, the capitalist world-system has been structured into two distinct spatial forms. The economy – i.e. production and trade – is organized into *spaces of flows* (a term originally coined by Manuel Castells [1983] and now commonly used to describe network-like spatial forms), through a unified and global division of labour supported by trans-national commodity chains. The political – that is, the regulation of society

---

6. World-systems analysis is a macro-historical approach to the development of cap-italism. According to it, the capitalist world-system emerged as a Europe-centric world economy in the sixteenth century. Its *raison d'être* is to promote the endless accumulation of capital, to which all contribute who produce for the capitalist world market. Phases of growth within the capitalist world-system are marked by the geo-graphical expansion of the capitalist division of labour, the increase in production capacities, and the increasing penetration of all social relations with capitalist logic. This process of spatial and social expansion of capitalism is a polarizing one and hence tied to a deepening of inequalities on different scales.

– is, however, organized into *spaces of territories*, through an inter-state system with many different nation states whose institutions (e.g. legislature and executive) are territorially bounded. The point of the bifurcation of the geography of the capitalist world-system into "a single division of labor but multiple polities and cultures" is that it creates the basis for the "appropriation of surplus of the whole world-economy by core areas" (Wallerstein 1974a: 391, 401), i.e. for uneven development. The reason for this is that the differentiation of the rewards (capitalists' profits and workers' remunerations, but also labour rights, etc.) that exist for different inputs in commodity chains at certain stages of production cannot be explained by properties of the production process itself (e.g. by different productivity), but rather by how much competition the respective inputs are exposed to in their production. The rule of thumb is the less competition, the more core-like a product is, generating higher profits and paying workers higher remuneration. Accordingly, capitalists are, in spite of all the rhetoric, not striving for a market economy, but, on the contrary, for protection from it and its competition, namely through the establishment of monopolies or quasi-monopolies. Protection from competition is attainable basically through state or state-supported measures like licensing, product and labour standards, import restrictions, and, most importantly, patents that warrant monopolies (see Chapter 5). However, not all states are equally capable of protecting "their" capitalists. Economically powerful ones, equipped with innovative companies, a strong currency, institutions able to act and, as a last resort, a military that radiates threat, can help corporations to achieve monopolies or quasi-monopolies more easily than weaker states. Consequently, the profitability of a product and the remuneration for the workers producing it essentially depend on the strength of the state at the respective production stage. Now, if the political were not organized in an inter-state system with many different states, each with a different strength to impose monopolies, but were global, like the division of labour, then the differentiation of protection from competition and thus the gradation of profit opportunities would be more difficult, if not unenforceable.

Because the political and economic strength of states has direct material consequences for producers and workers alike, "core" (or "centre") and "periphery" are not spatial metaphors, allegories to symbolize the geographies of the social relations of exploitation. Nor are they merely conceptual or abstract categories for structuring analysis. Rather, core and periphery refer to concrete places and concrete people, to socio-spatial realities, to "geographico-economic zones" (Wallerstein 1983: 28) within the capitalist world-system, created by the regionalization of core and peripheral activities, connected through surplus flows and identifiable by where (most of) the winners and (most of) the losers of capitalism live and work.

By not treating "the economy" and "the geography" as worlds apart, and by neither being content to simply locate economic activities in space, but by showing that the spatial structuring of the relations of production shapes their nature (and thus co-determines who belongs to the winners and who to the losers of the capitalist division of labour), world-systems analysis represents a truly spatialized political-economic analysis of capitalism. This is an important prerequisite for arriving at a citified analysis of uneven development, because it recognizes, first, that uneven development is organized (rather than simply happening, as a side effect of capital's spatially bound but unequally distributed self-expansion) and, second, that geography plays an important role in this organization, in the sense that capitalist actors rely on spatial strategies to maximize their profits. What remains unexposed in world-systems analysis, however, is that a comprehensive exploration of how accumulation is organized across and through particular geographies would need to include an examination of the places from which this occurs. Only in this way could we arrive at a citified analysis of uneven development. However, most world-systems analysis scholars pay little or no attention to cities, a fact that has been critically noted several times over the years (Smith 2003; Taylor 2013) but unfortunately still holds true. I shall return to this topic in Chapter 5. In the next chapter, however, I shall address the genius of cities, its foundations and the effects attributed to it in urban studies. The exceptionality of cities resulting from this genius is, after all, what underlies the claim that we need a citified analysis of capitalism.

CHAPTER 3

THE GENIUS OF CITIES

Cities, writes Storper (2013: 9), have a particular genius, which arises from their specific "behavioral context in which different elements of know-how come together... [creating] many overlapping worlds of face-to-face contact, [and] giving them a 'buzz'". As explained earlier, Storper's portrayal of cities as engines of economic growth and social advance is developmentalist, praising their efficiency while downplaying their role in uneven development as side effects of overall growth. The aim of this book is to challenge this one-sided enthusiasm for cities' productivity and to re-establish a critical analysis of their role in capitalism.

Before that, however, we have to ask ourselves where cities' extraordinariness comes from. If we do not assume that city dwellers are innately smarter and harder working by disposition than people in less populated areas, then what might the secret behind the economic power of cities be? Building on arguments from different currents in urban studies, cities' exceptionality can be conceptualized through three characteristics, which, in this combination, are unique to cities and which can therefore rightly be described as being "intrinsically urban in character" (Scott & Storper 2015: 9), namely agglomeration economies, being a node in various inter-city networks, and a massive built environment. In this chapter I will assess these elements, in order to lay the urban-theoretical foundations of my argument. The first step, however, must be to address an even more fundamental question, namely: what is a city? Is there such a thing as the "nature" of cities, features that characterize cities across time and space? Are all cities equal?

WHAT IS A CITY?

Any discussion about what a city is needs to start with a clarification of what is meant by "space", because cities are spatial things. Today, a relational interpretation of space dominates in the social sciences (and especially in the critical ones): space is no longer perceived in the Newtonian sense as an abso-lute *a priori* given substance, because such a view reduces space to a mere container of social processes, without any connection to them or meaning for them. A more appropriate representation of what constitutes space is a relational one, which goes back to Gottfried Wilhelm Leibniz (1646–1716). In this interpretation, space is not a pre-existent entity divorced from what is going on in societies, as their mere stage. Rather, the assertion is that space is *produced* through social practices and relationships, and that these spaces in turn reshape these social practices and relationships.

Such a conceptualization allows for a spatialization of social analysis as well as for the socialization of geography because it poses an indissoluble, two-way connection between "the spatial" and "the social". Firstly, space is, as French sociologist Henri Lefebvre argues in his ground-breaking book, *The Production of Space* ([1974] 1991), brought into being socially, not only through material practices (the erection of buildings or the assembling of objects, for example), but also cognitively, through perceptions and the attri-bution of meaning. The Brandenburg Gate in Berlin, for example, is not just a neoclassical monument, but serves as a "memory store" for German and European history. Secondly, socially produced spaces "matter", as Massey's (2005) powerful analysis puts it; they make a difference to the ways in which people act and how societies work: "It is not just that the spatial is socially constructed; the social is spatially constructed too" (Massey 1984: 6). Space is, thus, "a social product (or outcome) and a shaping force (or medium) in social life", as Edward Soja (1989: 7) summarizes. People make their history not *in* spaces, thought of as containers, but *through* them, thought of as means or vehicles. And people make their histories not through abstract space, but through specific real, concrete, tangible, lived spatializations – what Bernd Belina (2013) calls "spatial forms". He names four of them: territory, place, scale and networks. I am adding agglomeration to this list as a fifth important spatial form. All arise from social practices and relationships, while also being tied to physical-material environments and charged with meanings. And all of them react back on the societies that have produced them.

Conceptualization of space as both socially produced and socially effective is critical for my understanding of the nature of cities. If we want to under-stand cities' proactivity in uneven development then we have to think of urban space as the result as well as the medium of social action. Accordingly, in defining cities we have to go beyond mere quantitative classifications (such as, a city being a settlement with more than 2,000 inhabitants) and simple descriptions (such as the listing of certain features found in cities). Although it is true that cities throughout history are characterized by the concentration of functions such as political power, religious authority, production and trade, science, education and culture, there is a more fundamental question: why are all these functions exercised *from* cities? What do cities provide that enable certain actors to wield power and authority, to develop new products, services or processes? What, in a nutshell, makes cities more enabling environments that stimulate innovation than other conurbations?

It is noteworthy that we all are familiar with cities, intuitively recognizing what makes them special, but still have difficulty in rendering a clear definition of them. Across social science, people have grappled with the question of what a city is, and many have conceded that it is a difficult problem to solve. Yet, browsing through the literature, it is striking that many attempts to define the city revolve around similar notions. "Cities are places where a certain *energized crowding of people* takes place", says architectural historian Spiro Kostof (1991: 37; emphasis added), whereas Massey contends that "what we decided was that the crucial word for us [in defining cities] over and over again was intensity, that cities were actually intensities, *spatial intensities of social relations*" (1999: 76; emphasis added). "Energized crowding" and "spatial intensities" both suggest that what constitutes a city revolves around a certain quality of life that arises from many people living and working in close proximity. Of course, when viewed in detail, each city is unique. Nevertheless, most of what has been written about cities indicates that density and diversity are common denominators, a peculiarity that is common to all cities across space and time. Whereas density means that many "things" – people and their relationships to each other, their experiences, knowledge, thoughts and skills; goods and services; money; and physical artifacts – come together in a relatively small space, diversity implies that the "things" coming together are different and, importantly, will remain so (at least for a while). The genuine *urban* character of these two properties – density and diversity – is a leitmotif of urban research since its inception.

Louis Wirth (1938: 8), a key proponent of the Chicago School of Urban Sociology, defined the city as "a relatively large, dense, and permanent settlement of socially heterogeneous individuals", whereas Lewis Mumford ([1938] 1970: 3), an American polymath, sees the city as "the point of maximum concentration for the power and culture of a community . . . The city is the form and symbol of an integrated social relationship: it is the seat of the temple, the market, the hall of justice, the academy of learning. Here in the city the goods of civilization are multiplied and manifolded . . . [h]ere is where the issues of civilization are focused". For Braudel (1984: 180), cities are marked by a "high-voltage economy", whereas Lefebvre ([1970] 2003: 117) contends that the city "centralizes creation". Jacobs' (1961: 30) account focuses on cities' social heterogeneity as their defining feature: "Great cities are not like towns, only larger. They are not like suburbs, only denser. They differ from towns and suburbs in basic ways, and one of them is that cities are, by definition, full of strangers". In a similar vein, Richard Sennett ([1977] 2002: 39), one of the most important contemporary theorists of cities and public life, claims "that a city is a human settlement in which strangers are likely to meet. For this definition to hold true, the settlement has to have a large, heterogeneous population; the population has to be packed together rather densely; market exchanges among the population must make this dense, diverse mass interact".

Another word for density and diversity is agglomeration, which according to the *Oxford English Dictionary* (2022) is a "mass or assemblage", formed by "a process by which separate particles or elements collect together" and create a "union or approximation, often without assimilation". The crucial thing about agglomerations is that this assemblage of separate elements, which meet without merging, produces a particular setting, a "behavioral context" (Storper 2013: 9) for social actors which, according to this author, evokes something very specific, namely the *"genius of cities"*. I adopt Storper's notion of genius, but to agglomeration as its foundation I add two more elements, namely inter-city networks and the built environment. Like agglomeration, both are common to all cities across time and space (see later sections of this chapter).

In addition to Storper's thinking, my understanding of what the "genius of cities" means is influenced by the notion of *genius loci*, which in ancient Rome denoted a guardian spirit or god associated with a specific place. In modern times, *genius loci* is more generally associated with the atmosphere or spirit of a particular place, which gives it a distinctive character that makes (and marks) a difference to other places. The key point here is the notion that the qualities of a place, which constitute its atmosphere, matter to those who live and work there. Experiencing and absorbing a place's spirit, people are influenced by it. Accordingly, and consistent with the above reflections on space, the *genius loci* is a medium of social action and interaction, a means of social development. Two further aspects are important: as the particular spirit of a place, the *genius loci* cannot be created intentionally – it results from multidimensional and intersecting processes and relationships that occur. Nor can the *genius loci*'s impact be monopolized: it is a common good, from which nobody can be purposely excluded (except through exclusion from or denied access to a specific place; Vecco 2020).

Although it is common to associate the *genius loci* with specific places rather than with cities, it is not essential. In a geometric conception, a place is defined by its georeferenced coordinates, which can be large or small in size. Where the meanings ascribed to a locale make what a place "is", there is even less need to think automatically of a defined area of land. When we speak of the genius of Vienna at the turn of the nineteenth and beginning of the twentieth century, then one of the world's intellectual capitals, we are not just referring to a handful of addresses such as Neuwaldegger Straße 38 (where Ludwig Wittgenstein grew up), Berggasse 19 (where Sigmund Freud's couch stood), Hietzinger Hauptstraße 101 (where Egon Schiele had his last studio), Lothringerstraße 6 (home of Karl Kraus), or the Café Central, which was frequented by all of them and many other intellectuals, including Leon Trotsky (reputedly one of the best chess players in town). Rather, we are talking about a certain atmosphere *that hung over the city*, described as restless, pulsating, energetic, thought-provoking, that was nurtured by and in turn nurtured all these people, their activities and their relationships. However, neither the outer borders of this atmosphere can be precisely identified (certainly they were not identical with the administrative borders of Vienna), nor is it true that "the winds of intellectual advance" (Vance cited in Kostof 1991: 41) blowing through the city caught all of its residents: Adolf Hitler, for example, who lived in a men's hostel in the Meldemannstraße from 1910 to 1913, escaped it.[7]

With that in mind, I conceive of cities as socio-spatial units which are first of all characterized by a vibrant, animated and stimulating ambiance. This inspiring atmosphere arises from agglomeration, a particular mix of people, from human actions and relationships formed under the conditions of density and diversity. Actions and relationships grow from constant encounters with the new, the unfamiliar, from being exposed to the unknown and to the stranger. However, in order for agglomeration to develop and endure, two further ingredients are needed, namely the embeddedness of a locale into networks across space which connect to other cities, and the existence of physical infrastructure – the built environment – at a certain extent and scale.

Cities' density and diversity result from the bringing together of many different people, goods, ideas, and so on, and this bringing-together should be taken literally. Historically, cities have usually developed at junctions of traffic and trade routes, and this is no coincidence. The very concept of "city" (a place where strangers meet, in Sennett's words, a place that centralizes creation, according to Lefebvre) implies that cities emerge as nodes of multiple material and non-material flows, of links between people and buildings, which geographically are spanned over different distances – from the

---

7. Hitler, however, was immersed in another atmosphere, which also hung over the city, namely the pan-Germanist, nationalist and anti-Semitic voices and movements which made up the other side of the famous *fin-de-siècle* Vienna (Hamann 2011).

immediate hinterland to the end of the world. When agglomeration is aptly described as the "nature of cities" (Scott & Storper 2015), then it is equally correct to point to inter-city *networks* as the "'second nature' of cities". As Peter Taylor (2004: 1f.) contends: "There is no such thing as a single city operating on its own; cities come in packs". Without a network of cities, there would be no agglomeration because it is the connections to other cities which create the "bridges" over which everything flows into cities.

Yet, a city could not function as a node where everything is brought together without the corresponding physical infrastructure. There is, of course, the very obvious – a city *is* its buildings, streets, bridges and monuments. But there is also less obvious, but no less important, physical infrastructure: Gray Brechin (2006: 16), in his description of how much the city lives on the country (and actually, through the destruction of the country), points to a specific type of building as *the basis of all urbanization and the civilizations associated with it*, namely warehouses: "Within the city wall, granaries provided a measure of security never before available to nomadic tribes – a reservoir of calories to drive human and animal labor, which in turn could transform nature into finished goods, leisure into thought, and thought into technical innovations to yet further transform nature". Perhaps even more fundamental is William Cronon's observation that the built environment becomes humanity's second nature, designed to alleviate the adversities of the first (the "real") nature. To prevent Chicago from sinking into mud (the "natural" nature), in the 1840s the city was lifted and set onto new foundations: "[T]he new level of city streets came to seem quite natural for those who had gotten used to it, becoming yet another overlay of second nature in Chicago" (1991: 58). Accordingly, Mumford ([1938] 1970: 480) claims that across space and time, "[t]he essential physical means of a city's existence are the fixed site, the durable shelter, the permanent facilities for assembly, interchange, and storage". Referring to the capitalist city, Marxist geographer David Harvey (1985: 190) insists that "[i]t is impossible to imagine such a material process [like that of capital accumulation] without the production of some kind of urbanization as a 'rational landscape' within which the accumulation of capital can proceed. Capital accumulation and the production of urbanization go hand in hand". These quotes clearly show that the physical infrastructure, cities' built environments (by Harvey [*ibid*.: xv], too, called "second nature") matters because it provides the material basis on which all social processes and relationships that make up a city develop. So, it is not people or infrastructure in themselves that make up the genius of cities, but their interaction.

Cities share characteristics across space and time, which is why it is generic processes that drive the genius of cities. Nevertheless, one question remains: how to delimit the city? This can be done by means of geographical boundaries (where does the city begin and end?), or, more difficult, qualitatively: are there certain thresholds for the properties mentioned to become "urban"? In both cases, the boundaries cannot be drawn exactly. Rather, it is a matter of transitions, of converting quantity into quality, and there are certainly grey areas. The city, a socio-spatial unit with a particular atmosphere or genius, is always more or less, but never precisely, delineated. Yet, we instinctively know when we are in a city, or when something is missing that makes a city. Floridsdorf, for example, which administratively has belonged to Vienna since 1904, was not part of its *fin-de-siècle* dynamics, whereas the Semmering, a remedial-climatic health resort almost 100 km southwest of Vienna arguably was, because wealthy intellectuals enjoyed vacations there (Stefan Zweig's short story *The Burning Secret* gives a flavour of the resort). Yet, the problem that the boundaries cannot be drawn precisely does not matter, because, as Scott argues,

> if boundedness and enclosure were a necessary condition of onto-logical integrity we would never, by analogy, be able to talk in a meaningful manner about any complex unit of space or time with blurred outer boundary zones such as a mountain versus a plain, a river versus the ocean, the stratosphere versus the troposphere, the spring versus the summer, or a white neighborhood versus an African-American neighborhood. What makes these phenomena ontologically distinguishable (and epistemologically knowable in realist terms) is that they possess coherence over some significant set of criteria that identify a meaningful constitutive inside. The existence or non-existence of a linear boundary is irrelevant to the presence or absence of this coherence. (2017: 32)

Cities have to be delimited in time, too, because *city-ness* is not something that is achieved once and for all. Here, the distinction Jacobs (1970: 50) makes between "city" and "town" is useful: "[C]ities are places where adding new work to older work proceeds vigorously. Indeed, any settlement where this happens becomes a city". A city is therefore a place that creates innovation, regardless of the number of inhabitants or an administrative-legal definition. Town-ness, on the other hand, implies repetition. Note, that for Jacobs the watershed does not run between growth and stagnation, but between creativity and routine, between innovation and replication. Detroit at the turn of the twentieth century is for Jacobs a city, whereas late-nineteenth-century Manchester is an example of a city on the way to town-ness, "the very symbol of . . . long and unremitting decline" (*ibid.*: 88). Although Jacobs does not introduce "hard", clearly measurable criteria for her distinction between "city" and "town", everyone familiar with the history and geographies of capitalism would intuitively agree with her assessment. City-ness is a matter of becoming and eventually passing away, which in the capitalist age is coupled with the spatial and temporal dynamics of capital accumulation.

This leads to another aspect: from Jacobs' distinction between city-ness and town-ness follows that there is a transition zone between the two, and also within each category. Accordingly, not all cities are the same (equally extraordinary, vibrant, important, etc.). Rather, it is reasonable to differentiate, not only between cities and non-cities, but also between more and less dynamic cities, between those cities that are taking the lead at a given point in time and those that are falling behind. Yet we should keep in mind that the transitions are gradual ("as a mountain versus a plain", in Scott's words), for which reason it makes little sense to specify an exact number of cities that have the genius. For a guestimate, however, it is interesting to mention that the Globalization and World Cities Research Network (GaWC), a research network for the study of global cities, currently speaks of 525 such cities – from Aberdeen and Abidjan to Zhuhai and Zurich – (Taylor *et al.* 2010a), whereas the consulting agency McKinsey denotes 600 cities as the backbone of the world economy (Dobbs *et al.* 2011). The matching order of magnitude may be coincidental, but it is certainly interesting. The large number and the geographical dispersion of cities, which form the economic backbone of the world economy, also show that the separation into ordinary cities and global cities is both impossible and makes little sense. So, while my argument about the Janus-facedness of the genius of cities concerns a generic process, when it comes to operationalizing research on this topic, I would suggest starting with one of these 500–600 cities.

One very last point: assuming a genius of cities implies a relational understanding of space, which I introduced at the beginning of this chapter. Yet, the idea that the capitalist relations of production "are *simultaneously* social and spatial", both "space-contingent" and "space-forming" (Soja 1980: 208, 211; emphasis added) has been controversial since it came up. Soja's (*ibid.*: 219) notion of an "explicit spatial problematic" in capitalism has been criticized as "spatial fetishism" – the imbuing of space with social effectiveness, the "making social relations between people appear as relations between places or spaces", as Harvey ([1982] 2006: 338) put it. Harvey (*ibid.*) and other Marxist geographers doubted that it was correct "to consider antagonisms between spatial categories, such as town and country, city and suburb, developed versus 'Third World' and so on, as important attributes of capitalism". According to the critics, such views run the risk of reifying space, of treating it as autonomous from or exogenous to social processes.

Speaking of a genius of cities bears the same danger. It is therefore necessary to emphasize that although cities have a certain genius, they do not act. Their genius refers to a specific socio-material environment which sends "messages, . . . suggestions" for human action (Jacobs 1970: 59), but which does not determine what these actions should be for or against. This is what people decide, alone and in various forms of associations (e.g. firms, political movements), and, importantly, "not under circumstances of their own choosing, but under immediately encountered, given and transmitted circumstances", as Marx wrote ([1869] 1960: 115; own translation). Among these circumstances is the city.

The discussion about spatial effectiveness versus spatial fetishism boils down to matters of philosophy of science, namely whether space is an actor or a social structure, and how structure and action relate to each other. I think of cities as socio-spatial structures of society, conceived of as sets of relations between objects and social practices. The landlord–tenant relation, for example, is such a structure, because it presupposes many "things" that transcend the personal relationship between the respective individuals: the existence of material objects (e.g. houses); the legal institution of private property, which allows certain individuals to dispose of these material objects as they see fit, and which is widely accepted (so that the police does not have to protect every house from misappropriation by non-owners); a distribution of income and wealth which allows some to own real estate and others not; the capitalist drive for profit; urban segregation, which determines (and is determined by) the amount of profit to be made with a specific property; etc. (Sayer 2010: 63). Such structures are real, they exist in their material and social dimensions, regardless of whether we can see and observe them directly (as we usually can't tell by seeing people if they are landlords or tenants), and regardless of how they are perceived (whether I think private property is good and you think it's bad, does not immediately, in the epistemological process of perception, change the landlord–tenant relationship as it really exists). However, although social structures exist independently of individual persons, they are produced, reproduced and transformed by people – they "exist only in virtue of, and are exercised only in, human agency" (Bhaskar [1979] 2005: 44). Because of the necessity to be reproduced through human practices, social structures are open to change. People are not doomed to reproduce social structures in the sense that they remain the same forever. However, while social structures can be changed, such changes take time because structures are, as Roy Bhaskar (*ibid.*: 42) put it, "relatively enduring". Moreover, social structures have a recursive relationship to human activities, shaping and being shaped by them. Society pre-exists the existence of an individual human, its structures are influencing any human activity, in the constraining as well as enabling sense. Accordingly, social structures have causal power for concrete actions (if I have to rent my housing, for example, I necessarily have to earn the money for it). Finally, although social structures and human agency are interwoven, they must be kept apart analytically. Structures operate differently than individual actions, they have different properties, and we choose different terms for each realm: when talking about people, agency and practices, we use words like strategy, intention, responsibility or sense of justice, whereas when referring to social structures we use market mechanisms, accumulation dynamics or rent gap (Pühretmayer 2013).

In sum, conceiving of cities as socio-spatial structures helps to avoid the trap of spatial fetishism. Cities do not act themselves, but they – or their genius – provide a specific setting which offers incentives for action. The direction of those actions induced by the city environment, however, is open – creativity can serve the development of climate-neutral techniques as well as that of financial instruments used for predatory lending (for example, the subprime system in the early 2000s in the US and elsewhere) based typically on unfair, misleading and abusive credit terms.

EXTERNALITIES RESULTING FROM AGGLOMERATION

In the previous section, I defined cities as places that are, regardless of differences in time and space, characterized, among other things, by an extraordinary density and diversity of social relationships and physical artifacts. Their specific material, social and intellectual environments have made cities historically into centres of political power and domination, of ceremonial and religious authority, of artisanal production (especially for high quality goods and military equipment), later of industry and, of course, of trade. Cities *are* the market: they concentrate production and purchasing power, they provide the material infrastructure for exchange (hence market*place*, which has an obvious physical connotation), and they organize "external" trade with other cities. "The city", writes Lefebvre (2003: 117), "brings together whatever is engendered somewhere else, by nature or labor: fruits and objects, products and producers, works and creations, activities and situations . . . It centralizes creation".

The term "agglomeration" denotes this bringing together of different people, products, skills, money, relationships, knowledge, etc., in a confined space. It refers to a specific socio-spatial structure that is capable of producing special effects due to the density and diversity of social actors. These effects are called externalities – consequences of an activity that affects other parties without their having been involved in the activity itself. "Agglomeration economies" belong to these externalities. They are not the direct result of economic activity itself, but of its spatial concentration. Although this notion applies in principle to both positive and negative externalities, in economic geography and in urban studies above all the positive dimension is emphasized, namely, the advantages that arise for companies from co-locating with other firms in cities. Agglomeration engenders increasing returns, and because of these *internal* dynamics of urban economies, cities' economies grow faster than those in other places, and some cities' economies faster than others'. The study of agglomeration economies is therefore always indirectly also a study of uneven development, as we have seen in the discussion of the differentiated growth model, which in Storper's version, for example, is based on the notion of agglomeration economies.

Reflections on the positive effects of the geographical concentration of economic activities accompany thinking about cities since the ancient Greek philosophers Plato and Xenophon. Adam Smith also argued that the expansion of the market that occurs in the course of urbanization and the growth of cities, enables and requires a deepening of the division of labour, which in turn engenders economic progress – Smith's famous *Wealth of Nations* (1776). Among the first to systematize thoughts about the positive effects of agglomeration on economic development were the economists Alfred Marshall (1842–1924) and Alfred Weber (1868–1958). Marshall coined the term "industrial districts" to denote dense local networks of (mostly) small firms, which specialize in similar products. Key is the notion that the spatial and social proximity of economic actors in industrial districts fosters innovation because, "[g]ood work is rightly appreciated, inventions and improvements in machinery, in processes and the general organization of the business have their merits promptly discussed: if one man [sic] starts a new idea, it is taken up by others and combined with suggestions of their own; and thus it becomes the source of further new ideas" (Marshall 1920: 271). By spilling over from one to the other, even among competitors, knowledge multiplies as if by itself – it is, as Marshall's famous phrase goes, "as it were in the air". Alfred Weber ([1909] 1922) saw the emergence of vast industrial cities in Germany in the early twentieth century as the result of so-called "agglomerative factors". He argued that the geographical concentration of economic actors and their activities in cities result in productivity gains for all because due to the size of markets, inputs such as technical equipment or labour become more easily available, so that it reduces the costs of their procurement. Clustering of industrial activity also reduces the costs of transport and storage.

Gilles Duranton and Diego Puga (2004) identify three interrelated "fundamental" activities that produce the economic advantages of the agglomeration: sharing, matching and learning. Sharing refers to what in economics is called "indivisibility": the costs of infrastructures (such as roads), public goods (such as security) and services (such as schooling) are high, but they are difficult to allocate to specific users. Agglomeration offers a way out: the more people who use a street, enjoy public security or attend school, the cheaper their provision becomes per capita. Risk is also shared in agglomerations. The larger a labour market, for example, the safer investment in the training of a specialized worker becomes, because the likelihood of finding a company that needs his or her particular knowledge is higher. Finally, the advantages that the specialization in advanced divisions of labour bring about are also shared: when productivity increases in the production of one commodity, the price goes down for everyone who needs that commodity as an input. The second activity is matching. The larger a market, the greater the chance that supply and demand will correspond. In a large and diversified labour market, for example, search time and, consequently, costs decrease, and workers find (other) employment more easily. Specialized professions (such as patent attorneys, for example) also need sufficient demand in order to be profitable, and this is easier to find in (big) cities. Finally, Duranton and Puga (*ibid.*) identify learning as the third activity producing agglomeration externalities. Because "learning is a form of interaction" (Storper 2013: 96), the bringing together of many and varied face-to-face contacts creates the specific "behavioural context" already referred to. The advantage lies not so much in the enormous amounts of information available, but rather that through many contacts new, diverse and therefore non-standardized knowledge becomes accessible, which facilitates mediation and hence learning. Innovation, therefore, does not simply pop up in the laboratories or libraries of solitary geniuses, but arises when "ideas have sex", as the British zoologist Matt Ridley (2010) puts it. Because cities are contact-rich environments – full of "superadditive communication processes", as Storper (2013: 150) writes – they offer every opportunity for ideas to have sex. And that is exactly why innovation is intimately linked to cities. Personal interactions boost learning for two reasons. Firstly, they make tacit or "implicit" knowledge accessible, that is, knowledge embodied in people and rooted in their practices, experiences and contexts. Whereas explicit knowledge can be verbalized, codified, stored and shared over distance, tacit knowledge cannot. Access to it requires direct exchange in interpersonal networks and hence the co-localization of actors. Secondly, face-to-face interactions are usually "buzzing" (cf. *ibid.*): they are high-frequency, allow for quick feedback, and are enriched by visual and physical signals when probing and evaluating the interlocutor. This leads to results that cannot be achieved otherwise, namely the transfer and the *increase* of non-standardized, new knowledge.

For Storper (2013: 227), the "local genius" of cities develops from "strong forms of local interaction" which allow knowledge to circulate more easily, making it easier for ideas to be picked up and combined with other thoughts, which in turn fosters innovation. If we understand learning as a combinatorial activity, as a feedback process based on existing knowledge to which new ideas are added, then we easily recognize why cities are key to innovation: they provide the social and physical environment for knowledge sharing (as, for example, the Viennese Café Central at the *fin de siècle*). In other words, because of their density and diversity, cities permanently create *situations*, expressively defined by cultural theorist Lauren Berlant (2011: 5) as "a state of things in which something that will perhaps matter is unfolding amid the usual activity of life. It is a state of animated and animating suspension that forces itself on consciousness, that produces a sense of the emergence of something in the present that may become an event". Cities do just that. Because of their buzz, they generate and offer opportunities for anything to emerge. Or, as Lefebvre ([1970] 2003: 129) writes: "In urban space, something is always happening".

While there is solid empirical evidence that innovation (measured mostly by patent applications) is indeed concentrated in cities, and that this concentration increases with the size of cities (at least from the 1990s onwards; Bettencourt *et al.* 2007; Andrews & Whalley 2022), there is, however, some debate about the causality of the link between innovation and cities. For example, Richard Shearmur (2012: 9, 13), in a widely cited paper, expresses an "uncomfortable feeling" about the soundness of the empirical evidence for the almost commonsensical "idea that innovation processes are endogenous to regions or cities". Provocatively, Rune Fitjar and Andrés Rodríguez-Pose (2017) summarize this scepticism by alluding to Marshall's (1920: 271) famous phrase: "nothing is in the air". While Shearmur's (2012) reference to the importance of inter-city networks (and not just cities taken on their own) does not, in my view, reduce the centrality of the city for innovation (because cities and their exceptionality must always be conceptualized as resulting from networks; see next section), he also objects that innovation does not *per se* require urban environments because, as Ron Boschma (2005) has pointed out, too, geographical proximity is neither a necessary nor a sufficient condition for innovation. Other dimensions of proximity (such as social, organizational, cognitive, or institutional proximity) are additionally required or can even replace geographical proximity. However, Boschma also emphasizes that geographical proximity favours all other dimensions of proximity, which then again underlines the importance of the city. In my view, this understanding captures what Jacobs, Storper, and others who conceive of the city "as a machine for learning" (McFarlane 2011) mean when they speak of the city as a specific "behavioral context" (Storper 2013: 96) that "makes injecting improvisations . . . feasible. Cities . . . create that context. Nothing else does" (Jacobs 1985: 155). In sum, even if different authors weigh the "harder" agglomeration factors (such as infrastructures or labour markets) and the "softer" ones (a "buzzing", learning-inducing milieu) differently, there is a consensus that it is them that turn cities into "primary economic organs" (Jacobs 1970: 6).

EXTERNALITIES RESULTING FROM INTER-CITY NETWORKS

The genius of cities does not arise from the basis of agglomeration economies alone, it is also based on externalities stemming from cities' relationships with other cities. Spaces of flows which connect cities to other cities are indeed the prerequisite for localized agglomeration advantages to develop. Links to other cities are, per Taylor (2004: 1), "not an optional 'add-on' for theorizing the nature of cities, but the very *raison d'être* of cities". In a similar vein, Brian Berry contended that "[t]he most immediate part of the environment of any city is other cities" (1964: 160f.), whereas Jacobs (1970: 35) asserted that a "city seems always to have implied a group of cities". Doreen Massey, John Allen and Steve Pile conclude that "it is impossible to tell the story of any individual city without understanding its connections to elsewhere. Cities are essentially open; they are meeting places . . . [*t*]*hey pull into themselves*" (1999: 2; emphasis added). To prosper, cities need relations to other cities because through inter-city networks everything is provided that a city needs to develop: labour needed for economic expansion, capital seeking investment, information, or hitherto unknown skills, goods and services.

In inter-city networks, the nodes are formed by cities (or, if we change scale, by buildings or even the individuals located within them), whereas connections between them are created through physical links (such as highways, railways and fibre optic cables) and through flows which can either be non-material (e.g. some of today's money transfers, circulating information) or through the movement of material (e.g. commodities or people). Importantly, and so as not to personify cities, the agents of network formation are not the cities themselves, but people in them (Taylor 2004). Inter-city networks arise from the social activities and relationships, which they embody and consolidate. The most important network makers have always been economic actors. Merchants of the "Hanseatic League" in the European

High and Late Middle Ages spanned a close-knit network in northern Europe; Amsterdam's merchants organized the European grain trade in the sixteenth and seventeenth centuries, which connected hamlets, villages and towns in the Baltic, northwestern and southern Europe, and these via Madrid, Seville, Cadiz and Mexico City to the colonial silver-mining cities in central Mexico; in the eighteenth and early nineteenth centuries, chartered companies such as the East India Company made trade and inter-city networks global; in the past 50 years or so, the transactions of transnational corporations and of business (or producer) services firms have created a fully globalized network of cities, comprising 525 global cities (Taylor *et al.* 2010a) and countless other cities around the world where metals are mined, cars are assembled, and tourists are served. Migrants are also important network makers, as are mayors, municipal officers, planners and private consultants who do policy tourism in search of best practices. Over time, two important changes in inter-city network formation occurred: tangible dimensions of connections between cities (e.g. trade in goods) have lost importance in favour of intangible, virtual facets; and the number of cities integrated into networks has increased, and their geographical reach has enlarged.

To underscore the importance of inter-city networks for urban economies Taylor *et al.* (2010b) even speak of a "central flow theory". The argument is that positive economic externalities are not confined to agglomeration economies, but also result from being part of networks. The co-location of firms in dense environments is therefore only one source of cities' extraordinary dynamism, whereas the interaction of economic agents across space, namely between cities, is a further one. If being in the city facilitates sharing, matching and learning (Duranton & Puga 2004), then being networked has the same effect. Economic agents in interlinked cities benefit from what William Alonso (1973) has called "borrowed size" – through network connections, cities can access other cities' agglomeration economies. Such "urban network externalities" (Camagni & Salone 1993) increase with the number of participants (firms) and nodes (cities). The more people feed knowledge into a network, the more knowledge is shared, and the more cities participate in the network, the wider the geographical basis of this knowledge inputs and dissemination becomes.

Accordingly, agglomeration economies are the result of networking activities across space. Cities' local "buzz" (Storper & Venables 2004) is not just a local affair. It requires what Bathelt *et al.* (2004) have called "global pipelines" to be set in motion. To grasp why inter-city networks are so critical to local development, it is once again helpful to refer to Jacobs, and in particular to a process she calls the "[r]eplacement of imports". It works like this: a city imports certain goods from another city, but after a time the people there start to manufacture the previously imported goods themselves. Yet, their product is not a simple copy of the formerly imported good, but an adapted, enhanced, *improved* version. This probably small modification is what makes the difference: according to Jacobs, a copy would simply lead to growth – more of the same – while making an improved product means development, because a new good has been added to the existing ones. This has various effects: firstly, production of a previously imported good generates new work, and by doing so it diversifies the local economy and makes the division of labour more complex. Secondly, the funds that previously had to be spent to import a good, are now available for new imports. Accordingly, and thirdly, a city that replaces imports not only develops its own economy: by increasing the demand for other cities' products, the replacement of imports also contributes to the growth of other urban economies. For Jacobs (1970: 167), this "powerful multiplier effect of the replacement process" is the fundamental principle for economic development, and it requires connections between cities. Therefore, it is appropriate to denote inter-city networks as cities' "second nature" (Taylor 2004: 2).

From the complementarity of relationships between cities proposed by Jacobs, she and others conclude that cities' external relations to other cities are horizontal (rather than hierarchical) by nature. In a widely cited paper, Roberto Camagni and Carlo Salone (1993: 1054, 1059) claim for example, that the original meaning of networks is "economic 'equipotentiality' and horizontal links in spatial relationships". Therefore, the term "city network" should be reserved for "systems of relationships and flows, of a mainly horizontal and non-hierarchical nature among specialised centres". In my view, the claim that relationships between cities are in essence non-hierarchical, is certainly very debatable. Of course, there are many good examples of the horizontal nature of city networks: one, which advantages everyone who participates in the network, is the history of the spread of financial innovations. In the early modern period, writes Braudel (1983: 556), financial innovations "spread from city to city", distributed by merchants, who, travelling around, could not, as in the case of the bill of exchange, "have failed to notice this convenient method of transferring a sum of money to distant parts simply by a piece of paper". Yet, while it is true that the spread of financial innovations "from city to city" benefitted merchants moving in inter-city networks (as well as capitalism as a system!), it certainly did not benefit all people, neither in the cities in question nor (and even less) in their near and far hinterlands. I shall come back to this aspect of the alleged non-hierarchical complementarity later (see Chapter 4).

EXTERNALITIES RESULTING FROM BUILT ENVIRONMENT

I have emphasized that the external economies of agglomeration and of inter-city networks are related to each other – urban density and diversity would not exist without cities' external connections to other cities, while urban networks would be pointless if they did not serve as pipelines through which one city can borrow other cities' size and participate in their density and diversity. Agglomerations and inter-city networks, however, do not develop out of thin air, nor are they purely abstract environments. Rather, their social effectiveness unfolds in and through physical environments – houses, factories, streets, offices, markets, fibre optic cables, stock exchanges, radio masts, airports, etc. Although it is true that the clustering of economic activities in relatively small spaces – cities – and the flows of goods, people, money, etc., between them – inter-city networks – boost innovation, productivity and economic output, it is important to remember that agglomerations as well as urban networks both require and produce specific built environments.

Building on an understanding of space as an active moment in, rather than a passive container of, society (see first section of this chapter), Harvey (1985: xv, 190) asserts that "capitalism creates a physical landscape of roads, houses, factories, schools, shops, and so forth in its own image . . . Capital accumulation and the production of urbanization go hand in hand".[8] Accordingly, it is through the physical, yet socially produced urban landscapes that cities acquire their agglomeration and networks externalities. Command over the built environment is therefore the third source of cities' genius.

The term "built environment" refers to the materiality of spaces created by humans for their activities. In economic terms, agriculture needs fences, barns and warehouses; manufacturing needs factories and power stations, services need shops and office buildings. All sectors need streets and railway lines on which products are brought to the consumers and, of course, houses in which the workers live, schools and universities where they are trained, and hospitals in which they are born and where they are cared for in the event of illness. Cities, as "intense emplacement[s] of buildings" (Walker 2016: 171), are therefore the "natural ecosystem" for the economy, they provide

---

8. Harvey also stresses that the built environment is impregnated with the contradictions inherent in capitalism. While capital needs to be mobile and seeks to reduce turnover time, the built environment is spatially immobile, long-lived and difficult to alter. For reasons of brevity, and because the aspect of contradictions embodied in the capitalist built environment is not of central importance for the argument of this book, I shall not pursue this aspect any further here.

"a spatially specific resource complex of humanly created assets to support both production . . . and consumption" (Harvey 1985: 144). Although every society needs physical infrastructure for production, circulation and consumption, Harvey (e.g. 1985, 2006) has pointed out repeatedly that in the context of the capitalist mode of production[9] command over localized complexes of human-made physical resources takes on a new quality – it is the *sine qua non* of accumulation. It is therefore not only that capital increasingly urbanizes – the "centralization of capital finds its most accomplished geographical expression in urban development" (Smith ([1984] 2008: 181) – but also that urban development – and, as part of it, the built environment – enables, accelerates and expands accumulation dynamics. This issue is of utmost importance for an understanding of the relationships between cities, their built environment and uneven development.

Consider, for example, the case of Detroit, the birthplace of Fordism, which shaped capitalism from the 1920s to the late 1970s. Fordism's technological heart was the moving assembly line, installed for mass production for the first time by the Ford Motor Company in order to produce the Model T. The moving assembly line, itself a part of the built environment, entailed, however, the production of a new factory landscape. It required much more continuous work space than was common in factories at the beginning of the twentieth century. Space requirements were further increased by another of Henry Ford's innovations in work organization, namely to integrate as much as possible of the entire supply chain on one site. Thus, in order for the dawning age of Fordist mass manufacturing to materialize and Detroit to become the world capital of automotive industry and thereby "the quintessential American city" (Stanley & Smith 1992: 33), the city's built environment had to be adapted. To realize an industrial space to fit the requirements of Ford, the architect hired, Albert Kahn, shifted from masonry construction to reinforced concrete, which amongst other things allowed for vast areas of uninterrupted work space, equipped with strong and vibration-resistant floors. When the plant in Highland Park, Michigan, opened in 1910, it was the largest production facility in the world, employing about 13,000 workers and 15,000 machines, and containing not only the actual factory, but also offices, a power plant and a foundry (Hyde 1996).

---

9. In Marxist thought, the term "mode of production" denotes the ways in which a society organizes the production of goods and services. It is determined by the relationships of the forces of production (i.e., what is brought together in production, from land and raw materials, tools and machinery to human labour) and the relations of production (i.e. the relationships that people enter into in the processes of production, circulation and consumption).

It was through (and not merely in) Highland Park and, a decade later, the Rouge Complex, as socially produced spaces and as physical landscapes created by capital "in its own image", that Ford revolutionized automobile production and manufacturing as a whole. And Kahn's new factory architecture, which has been implemented in hundreds of factories over the years for Ford, General Motors, Chrysler, Packard and other car manufacturers, was just as decisive for Detroit's transformation into "Motor City" as Ford's technological and organizational innovations were. The term "Motor City" can therefore be understood in two ways: it refers to Detroit as the capital of automobile production, but also to the fact that Detroit's industry was the engine of the US and thus the world economy for some time. Of course, this also meant that it was the driving force behind an uneven development that accelerated during this period. For instance, at the global level US GDP per capita exceeded that of the world by a ratio of 3.6:1 in 1900, but by 1950 it had grown to 4.5:1, with Asia in particular falling behind, but also Africa, while Latin America was able to narrow the gap somewhat (Maddison Project Database 2020).

In this chapter I have examined the ideas common within urban studies that see cities as a central analytical category for understanding economic growth. There is a broad consensus in the literature that cities' exceptionality arises from three elements that are unique to them: density and diversity, i.e. agglomeration; being a node in various networks at different scales; and a massive built environment. Thanks to these resources, cities are deemed to be pro-growth. They are held responsible for the "good" innovation from which economic progress, social prosperity, democracy (and increasingly also climate neutrality) arise, which is why it is generally accepted that there is an "almost universal positive association" (Brockerhoff & Brennan 1998: 82) between urbanization and development. In the next chapter, I shall turn to work that, while by no means representing hate literatures on cities (cf. Taylor 2004) nor creating dystopian images, have elaborated that cities' genius has another side, that the resources of cities have always been used to organize capitalist exploitation and oppression.

CHAPTER 4

THE JANUS-FACED GENIUS OF CITIES

The central claim presented in this book is that cities are causally linked not only to development, but also to its unevenness. In today's urban studies, however, growth and exploitation are not linked to each other at all, just as if they were not structurally and necessarily connected in a capitalist world. By and large, cities have been divorced from the study of the asymmetrical relationships that constitute the capitalist division of labour at regional or global scales, with the result that their generative power seems to have nothing to do with the "bad" innovation that produces ever new methods and means of exploitation and oppression. The devices that are used for the appropriation of the fruits of other people's labour, for subjugation, warfare and environmental destruction seem to be orphaned; evil seems to come from nowhere. I have already quoted Jane Jacobs' (1970: 121) dictum that poverty has no causes, only prosperity, and that this comes exclusively from cities. In Jacobs, this coming "from cities" assumes two meanings: while the first is more descriptive topographical (cities as the places where economic development takes place; see Figure 1.1), the second is plainly analytical: cities generate economic development due to their very specific characteristics. Deeply committed to the latter perspective, Jacobs equates poverty with the lack of city-centred benefits, indeed with "citylessness". Without cities, she claims, "we'd all be poor ... All through organized human history, if you wanted prosperity, you've had to have cities" (Jacobs 1997). A similar association of poverty with "citylessness" – i.e. with the countryside, rurality and agriculture – can be found in the arguments of Martin Ravallion (2007: 15), former director of the World Bank's research department. Opposing the notion of an "urbanization of poverty", which contends that poverty is becoming an urban problem rather than a primarily rural one, he rhetorically asked: "Are poor people gravitating to towns and cities?" His provocative-sounding, but serious answer: "Yes, but maybe not quickly enough".

And indeed, with the urbanization of the world, extreme poverty has decreased significantly (for the following data, see Moatsos 2021; World Bank 2022). Whereas in 1820 about 90 per cent of the world's population lived in extreme poverty, today it is about 10 per cent (the World Bank sets the threshold for extreme poverty at $1.90 a day, in purchasing power parities).[10] Of course, up until about 1980 the decline in the share of the extremely poor in the world's population was accompanied by an increase in their absolute number, which rose to almost 2 billion. Yet, since 1980 even the absolute number of people in extreme poverty has fallen, to a little less than 750 million today. Moreover, moderate poverty ($5.50 a day) has also decreased slightly. While, given the immense riches produced daily, 750 million extremely poor people is still scandalous, the analytically important point here is that it is difficult to attribute the reduction in poverty directly, let alone exclusively, to urbanization. Much of it was achieved not *globally*, but in China, which is responsible for about 60 per cent of the worldwide reduction in extreme poverty. Urbanization – in 2021 about 63 per cent of China's population lived in cities, up from 18 per cent in 1978 – is certainly an important part of the tremendous economic and social dynamics that have gripped China since Deng Xiaoping initiated reform in 1978. But China's rise to the world's largest economy (when measured in purchasing power parities; otherwise the second largest) is by no means solely or even primarily attributable to urbanization, but the result of strategic economic planning and the rigorous implementation of policy priorities, what allowed for the taking advantage of global economic opportunities. The fact that the connection between urbanization and poverty reduction is not a compelling one can also be seen from the example of Latin America, where extreme poverty only slightly decreased in recent decades, despite a high level of urbanization. In addition, many recent publications (e.g. Piketty 2014; Chancel *et al.* 2022; von Arnim & Stiglitz 2022) show that the polarization of income and wealth is increasing significantly in rich, highly urbanized countries, accompanied by the impoverishment of considerable parts of the population.[11] In the United States, for example, at the beginning of the 1990s the income share held by the richest 10 per cent was 13.8 times larger than the income share held

---

10. Purchasing power parities (PPPs) are indicators of price-level differences across countries. PPPs indicate how many currency units of a particular country are needed to buy a particular quantity of goods and services.

11. Due to the strong increase in GDP per capita in China and India, which together account for slightly more than one third of the world's population, global inequality between countries has decreased. Within countries, however, it is increasing, and also globally, if not countries but all incomes are compared.

by the poorest 10 per cent; by the end of the 2010s, it was already 17.1 times as much. The same trend can be observed in other countries, for example, in Germany (from 6.2 to 8.1) and China (from 7.4 to 10.5). Moreover, according to the International Labour Organization, 50 million people were living in modern slavery worldwide in 2021, a number that has significantly risen since 2016. Women and children remain disproportionately at risk of living in slavery (ILO *et al.* 2022).

These few data should be enough to suggest that we live in a world full of poverty, inequality and exploitation. Does this misery really come from nowhere? Do we simply still have too few and too small cities, as Ravallion (2007) suggests? Is it really plausible that cities' generative power only produces good? Given the great importance attributed to cities for understanding economic development, why does this importance not apply for the "development of underdevelopment" (Frank 1969) too? As indicated, I am concerned by the developmentalism implied in "the city has triumphed" notion, which is reminiscent of the heyday of modernization theory in the 1950s and 1960s and its idea that all countries and societies could develop, i.e. ultimately become "rich", and that cities were vehicles of this modernization: the diffusion of innovation and economic growth should work through a country's (ideally well-balanced) urban hierarchy, trickling down from the top, from the largest metropolis to the smaller cities, towns and the countryside. While the more technocratic notion of a balanced urban hierarchy has lost ground in both scholarly and political debate, the one-sided positive connotation of cities and their persistent association with innovation, productivity and growth have returned to the centre of scientific debates and to the top of the agenda of international organizations. My rationale for objecting to this developmentalism is simple: in capitalism "growth" and "exploitation" are closely and structurally linked and asymmetrical relations are "endemic, not transitory, features of capitalist development" (Peck 2017: 7270). And, of course, it also applies to the role of cities in capitalist development that you cannot get the "bright sides" without the "dark sides". It is therefore mandatory not only to scrutinize the links between growth and exploitation, but also to examine the role of the city in *both*. Again, I claim that the genius of cities is Janus-faced.

What we need then is a *citified* perspective on poverty and exploitation, an analysis of the production and reproduction of uneven development through the lens of cities, an understanding of what the city and its inherent characteristics have to do with powerful economic and political actors' capabilities to shape the world in their favour – and only in their favour. What is at stake, then, is the elaboration of a citified political economy of uneven development. This builds on the aforementioned spatialized political-economic analysis, such as that found in Massey's ([1984] 1995) notion that the division of labour emerges as a specific spatialization of ownership and power relations, but advances it further by assuming that the asymmetrical relations of production that constitute capitalism are not only spatially structured, but *from cities*: formed in and maintained from cities, they are impregnated with the interests and strategies of powerful urban actors. A citified political economy of uneven development does not merely mean "adding" cities as just one further element to the complex geographies of production and commerce, but rather to examine uneven development from a "city perspective", to scrutinize through the lens of cities how the asymmetrical relationships of divisions of labour are produced and sustained. Such a citified perspective is actually inherent in the term "political economy" itself whose two words are derived from Greek: *oikonomos* is the management of a household, *polis* means city or city-state and *politiká*, affairs of the cities. These linguistic roots are commonly translated to mean how a *country's* economy is managed, although there is no need for such a methodological nationalization.

I shall keep the city as the perspective from which to analyse the management of the economy. Building on Scott and Storper's (2015: 9) distinction between issues found in cities and those which are *of* cities, in the sense of being "intrinsically urban in character", I contend that the complex organizational know-how that underpins the production and reproduction of uneven development (e.g. the exploitative organization of commodity chains) are not only created in cities, but emerge *from* cities, developed on the basis of their extraordinary social and physical environments (i.e. agglomeration, networks, the built environment). Thus, what constitutes the foundations of cities' exceptional capacities for economic development also provides the fertile ground for the means through which uneven development is accomplished. This notion has implications for the way cities are theorized – they should be conceived of as *proactive* nodes in asymmetric relations across space, with special attention given to what they are providing that enables economic elites to forge such effective weapons of exploitation.

I have developed my notion of the Janus-facedness of the genius of cities on the basis of a variety of work that approaches the role of cities in the economy and society from different theoretical, historical and geographical perspectives, and that in one way or another can contribute to answering the question raised by Bryan Roberts (1986: 459), namely "how cities and the classes within them achieve control over other regions". The historical perspective (the early modern city in Europe; cities in the Spanish colonies in Central and South America) and the geographical expansion (Central and South America) together underline my contention that the processes that produce the genius of cities – and therefore also its Janus-facedness – are generic to cities (at least those since the sixteenth century, which we can describe as capitalist cities). This is not to say that all cities have always and everywhere been equally important for the production of uneven development, but that cities share, across time and space, characteristics that make them (potentially at least) into proactive nodes in the asymmetrical relations of the capitalist division of labour. To support this argument, I shall discuss the debates on the role of cities in the transition from feudalism to capitalism in Europe, referring both to the literature that has come to be known as the "transition debate" and to the relevant thoughts of Adam Smith and Karl Marx. I shall also consider Fernand Braudel's assessments of a city-driven capitalism from the fifteenth to the eighteenth centuries along with discussions (mainly related to Latin America) of parasitic (capital) cities during the period of colonialism and the era of "catching-up" development in the mid-twentieth century. As diverse as these literatures are, they all explore how cities' properties have enabled elites in cities to draw resources from cities and rural areas in global or national peripheries, thereby challenging the consistently positive view that dominates today about the genius of cities.

CITIES AS VANGUARDS: EUROPEAN CITIES IN THE TRANSITION FROM FEUDALISM TO CAPITALISM

The rise of capitalism, its evolution out of European feudalism and its steps toward world domination, poses fundamental challenges for the history and theory of cities because they played a crucial role in this development. Whether one associates the emergence of capitalism with the increasingly global activities of merchants in the fifteenth and sixteenth centuries or with industrialization from the eighteenth century onwards, attention is immediately and necessarily focused on cities, namely on Genoa and Amsterdam as paradigmatic cases for the former, and on Manchester for the latter. From a theoretical point of view, two issues stand out, namely the relationships between cities and towns[12] and the larger political entities they are part of (fiefdoms, regions, states, empires), and the relationships between

---

12. Notwithstanding the distinction between "city" and "town" discussed in Chapter 3, these two terms are used synonymously throughout this chapter. The reason is that in the literatures I refer to here, both terms are used without further differentiation.

cities and towns and the country. The first question is essentially about the degree of autonomy of cities and their elites from secular and ecclesiastical authorities, the second about the character of the most fundamental of all divisions of labour, namely that between agriculture and *all* other economic activities. Both topics played an important role in the so-called "transition debate", a scholarly dispute over the causes of the transition from feudalism to capitalism in Europe that began in the 1940s and 1950s. Whereas Marxist economist Maurice Dobb emphasized causes endogenous to feudalism (basically a demographic crisis and class struggles between serfs and noblemen), also Marxist economist Paul M. Sweezy countered that external factors (such as the growth of cities in number, size and dynamics; the intensification of long-distance trade; the upswing of urban markets, an increasing monetarization of regional economies; and the need of monarchs to raise money for wars) had been instrumental in the decline of feudalism and rise of capitalism.

From the point of view of urban theory, the most important intervention was made by John Merrington (1975), who rejected the dualism often inherent to this discussion (feudalism as a static, largely immobile and narrow-minded rural subsistence economy, from which feudal lords squeezed out rents versus a dynamic, open, innovative capitalist urban market economy). Merrington argued that European medieval towns were both part of the feudal mode of production and transcended it. Medieval cities neither formed "non-feudal islands" in feudalist seas, nor were their growth and dynamics merely the dependent variable in the transition from one mode of production to another. Rather, cities and their "urban 'capitalism'" was, according to Merrington, "both internal and external to the feudal mode" (*ibid.*: 178).[13]

Cities, their networks, and the remarkable growth of both in number, size and density from the tenth century onwards *must* have been internal to feudalism because this was the order from which they emerged. According to Merrington, the new socio-political-economic dynamics and relationships that would henceforth become identified with cities developed out of one of the essential and peculiar characteristics of European feudalism, namely "the overall parcellisation of sovereignty". And he continues that "feudalism was the first mode of production in history to allow . . . an *autonomous structural place* to urban production and merchant capital" (*ibid.*: 178; emphasis added). Parcellization of sovereignty means that in feudalism society was not clearly

---

13. The trickiness of the debate can be seen in the fact that Merrington uses the term capitalism but puts it within quotation marks.

organized from top to bottom, with well-defined hierarchies and chains of command. Rather, it was "based on sovereignty 'in several degrees'" (*ibid.*), that opened up scope for smaller territorial units such as cities. According to British Marxist historian Perry Anderson, it was the feudal parcellization of sovereignty "*alone* [which] permitted the political autonomy of the towns and their emancipation from direct seigneurial or monarchical control" (1978: 193; emphasis added).

The revolution that took place in Europe in the Middle Ages was, thus, a political one: while economic features such as commodity production were germane to urban economies long before feudalism and beyond Europe, and while Asian cities at that time were bigger and more impressive, the thorough fragmentation of political authority and the associated decentralization of rule in very localized patron–client relationships were peculiar to Europe alone. This is what allowed cities to change the system from within: the parcellization of political power permitted their *autonomous* development, something that had never happened before and nowhere else:

> The fact that the largest mediaeval towns never rivalled in scale those of either Antiquity or Asian Empires has often obscured the truth that their function within the social formation was a much more advanced one. In the Roman Empire, with its highly sophisticated urban civilization, the towns were subordinated to the rule of noble landowners who lived in them, but not from them; in China, vast provincial agglomerations were controlled by mandarin bureaucrats resident in a special district segregated from all commercial activity. By contrast, the paradigmatic mediaeval towns of Europe which practised trade and manufactures were self-governing communes, enjoying corporate political and military autonomy from the nobility and the Church (Anderson 1978: 150).

The medieval European city developed under the protection of, in some cases was even promoted by, feudal lords, and was in some respects thoroughly feudal. Cities' privileges[14] are a classic example of this, because ultimately they were *granted* by princes, bishops or kings to the cities. Even

---

14. Cities' privileges were mainly related to sovereign functions such as law, the withholding of customs duties and the collection of taxes; migration policy concerning the mobility and the settlement of craftsmen; and economic functions such as the right to hold markets, to mine and sell metal ore, and even to brew beer.

the urban economic dynamic itself needed (at least initially) the feudal order. For merchants' profits, price disparities between regions were essential, because only these allowed the practice of buying cheap in one place and selling at a higher price in another. For such price disparities to exist and to continue to exist, the parcellization of sovereignty and, accordingly, of economic space was essential. According to Merrington, being internal to feudalism "was the *condition*" for cities' ability to become external to it (1975: 178; emphasis added). It was only the emergence of spaces with thinned-out political control that gave towns that certain freedom of action necessary to assume "a pivotal role . . . both in the demise of feudalism and in the rise of capitalism" (Katznelson 1994: 163).

What made it possible for cities to develop out of the rules and relations of feudalism? Anderson stressed, as already noted, the political dimension, that cities developed (incrementally rather than in revolutionary upheavals) into "self-governing communes, enjoying corporate political and military autonomy from the nobility and the Church" (1978: 150). And he continues:

The most mature form taken by this autonomy was the commune, an institution that is a reminder of the irreducible difference between town and country even within their feudal unity. For the commune was a confederation founded by an oath of reciprocal loyalty between equals: the *conjuratio*. This sworn pledge was an anomaly in the mediaeval world: for although the feudal institutions of vassalage and liegeancy had an emphatically mutual character, they were bonds of obligation between superiors and inferiors in an express hierarchy of rank. Inequality defined them even more than reciprocity. The urban *conjuratio*, founding pact of the commune . . . embodied a new principle altogether – a community of equals. (*ibid.*: 194; emphasis in original)

Of course, the everyday reality of medieval cities was characterized by inequality, too, because the confederation was limited, firstly, to *men*, second to men not in feudal bondage, and third to men with proven economic status (e.g. by capital that one possessed or by an apprenticeship or master crafts-man's certificate). Destitute men, women, servants and children remained excluded from this equality. Moreover, the conjuration model was geograph-ically restricted to the most advanced economic regions in Europe such as northern Italy, and later Flanders and the Rhineland. Nevertheless, and no matter how few these "equals" (privileged citizens, respectively) may have been, their pact marked a turning point in history. What began to emerge in the larger, economically most dynamic cities was a *collective behaviour of the urban elite* (within which merchants took a leading role), a unification of interests, loyalties and strategies, leading to common and concerted action. In this way, cities became collective actors, "a 'collective seigneur'",[15] as Merrington (1975) puts it, both in the self-perception of their elites and in the perception of others: "Townsmen form a social unit which, however internally divided, they and their neighbours feel to be distinct" (Reynolds 1997: 156).

That the urban elite began to act collectively signified an important step towards class formation, which for Marx required not only an objective material base (such as common economic conditions and interests), but also the more subjective dimension of becoming aware of these common conditions and interests, and of acting accordingly. Since in the High and Late Middle Ages the distinction between group (particular guilds, for example) and territorial identities (being a burgher of a particular city) was meaningless, the interests of influential citizens came to be equated with urban interests. The crucial conclusion is that cities' self-government was, at least until the twelfth century, a means and not an end in itself. It was not the quest for the right of association or democracy that drove burghers to strive for greater autonomy, but the wish "to run their own affairs for *themselves*", which arose out of "growing wealth" and "a new confidence" that comes from it (Reynolds 1997: 168; emphasis added). Disputes, for example, were not about political rights, but about the right to trade free of tolls and the right to sell goods; and about the right to be tried in the city's courts according to municipal customs (a right that implied protection from claims from outside the city).

How limited in scope and in geographical coverage this grant of political power to cities may have been, it was a key moment in the push for capitalism. Due to the fragmentation of authority within feudalism the socio-spatial units of property (people who possessed private means were able to appropriate what others had produced) and of political authority (people who had formal power over others) became identical (Katznelson 1994: 170). The moment, however, that this fusion of subordination and appropriation began to involve not only greater or lesser nobles acting according to the feudal logic of extracting rents from the peasantry, but also groups with genuine interest in *accumulation*, namely urban merchants – the moment in which the political chequerboard of feudalism consisted not only of fiefdoms, but also of self-governed cities – the meaning and implications of

---

15. *Seigneur* originally is a feudal title and refers to a person or collective who owned a form of land tenure as a fief, with all associated rights over person and property.

the feudal privatization of political power began to change fundamentally. While, in the short term, "the existence of this corporate urban autonomy as a 'collective seigneur' . . . encouraged the fullest development of merchant capital" (Merrington 1975: 178), in the medium term it triggered a process which was indispensable for the establishment of capitalism. According to Braudel, "[c]apitalism only triumphs when it becomes identified with the state, *when it is the state*" (1977: 64; emphasis added), and it was precisely this fusion of political and economic power that happened for the first time in the European medieval cities (particularly in northern Italy). As Arrighi (1994: 12) points out, this was a truly historic turning-point: "From this perspective, the really important transition that needs to be elucidated is not that from feudalism to capitalism but from scattered to concentrated capitalist power. And the most important aspect of this much neglected transition is the unique fusion of state and capital, which was realized nowhere more favorably for capitalism than in Europe".

To achieve sustained capital accumulation based on exploitation, urban elites developed common concerted actions to defend and expand their political and economic liberties not only against those "up there", that is, against the secular and ecclesiastical feudal authorities, from whom they wanted ever greater autonomy for less and less in return. Equally important was the fight against the rural producers and small-scale merchants below them, whose competition the urban elites sought to eliminate and from whom they sought to squeeze out more and more surplus. The strategy to achieve this consisted of a *combination* of free trade and monopoly policies – something that might seem contradictory to macroeconomic textbooks, but which is in fact a common and promising strategy in the history of (and in today's) capitalism (Arrighi 1994). Because the medieval towns were the first to apply this dual strategy of selective free trade and strategic monopolies on a larger scale, they served as "laboratories for the working out of techniques and practices of economic production and exchange" (Katznelson 1994: 184).

The right to trade free of tolls and the right to sell goods were key issues in cities' struggle for more autonomy. Pursuing free-trade policies expanded the sphere of action for city-based merchants and reduced costs incurred in buying or selling, and it helped to subdue the peasantry, whose economic spaces were penetrated. However, unrestricted free trade would have created markets, and markets always *imply competition*. In a market economy, the economically weaker can use their central strength – producing at lower costs – to contest the stronger. For the stronger, a real market is therefore a burden, threatening profits and forcing constant efficiency improvements. Accordingly, keeping potential rivals out through barriers to entry is more convenient, and one of the most effective entry barriers is legally protected monopolies (for further discussion, see Chapter 5). The crucial point now is that *medieval towns were born exactly as such monopolies*, as socio-territorial entities protected by feudal privileges and promoting the interests of merchants and guilds through *conditional* free trade. The monopoly, Hibbert claims, has been essential to the "existence" of medieval towns because they

> became distinctive economic and social units just when and because certain places were set apart and defended by laws or privileges making them market and production centres and denying some or all such rights to the countryside around. . . . They *were* because other places were not, they *had* because other places had not. They grew when and where lords restricted trade to a centre, granted special protection or privileges to those who settled or did their business at a defined place, gave a legal market to some locality and so denied some economic activities to everywhere else. *The monopoly belonged originally to a certain place rather than to certain people* . . . Non-residents might be allowed to import – but they imported to the town's market; they might have permission to export – they exported from the town's market; they might even, by 'gelding' with the inhabitants, participate in retail trade – at the legal market place and time. . . . *What was always intolerable was that the vital functions of the town should leak and diffuse over the countryside.* Of course, it was natural for a monopoly of trade at a place to become a monopoly of those who lived at that place and finally a control of all trade by the richer merchants among local inhabitants. (1965: 197f.; last two emphasis added)

Merrington (1975: 180) adds that it was precisely this "exclusivism . . . [which] must be seen as . . . the precondition for the development of merchant capital at this stage". Since merchants' core business was to buy low and sell high (e.g. grain), they depended on the freest possible access to as many farmers and their product and to as many hungry mouths as possible. This was why they sought an expansion of the market – the free trade motive. Yet, since merchants' profits depended on price differences between buying and selling, they needed to ensure both spheres remained separate – the motive to prevent free trade and the expansion of the market. The reason to create a partial – and not really free – market applies to craft products, too. Supplying them to the rural population required a market with as many buyers as possible, but doing so at excessive prices required a monopoly of supply, for which reason the development of a market for producers had to be prevented. By combining monopolies and free-trade policies, medieval towns were "incipiently mercantile. They provided protected and regulated economic environments for the elaboration of increasingly robust craft production and for the extension of networks of trade beyond the confines of the local region" (Katznelson 1994: 183). It was free trade behind entry barriers that made it possible for "the town . . . [to exploit] the land economically everywhere and without exception" because merchants' "commercial fraudulence" (Marx [1894] 1991: 937) – such as speculating on bad harvests, food shortages and rising prices – required free access to the fields and the crops of the peasantry, whereas the ability to charge usurious interest to nobles and rural debtors resulted from the opposite, namely the monopolistic control of money in general and credit in particular.

So, that cities could become a "vanguard force" (Anderson 1978: 192) of capitalism was based both on the countryside's partial inclusion in its economic realm and its partial exclusion from it. The exclusion of rural producers, however, did not mean that they were "isolated", but that they were forced out of (the more) profitable activities. This corresponds to the definition of peripheralization: the country was transformed from a sphere with wide-ranging production, including handicrafts, into agriculture and mining, and degraded to being a supplier of raw materials to the cities and a buyer of urban products. Cities in northern Italy, for example, where this process was set in train early on, "set out to conquer the surrounding countryside . . . a territorial *contado* from which the town could thereafter raise taxes, troops and grain to increase its own power and prosperity *vis-à-vis* its rivals . . . the intervening countryside . . . was annexed to the towns" (Anderson 1978: 166f.; emphasis in original).

Now, what did the intrinsically urban features cited as the basis of the genius of cities have to do with the fact that urban elites became able to develop common strategies and to achieve control over rural regions and their producers and workers? What enabled townspeople to exploit the opportunities offered by the feudal parcellization of sovereignty so that they became a force external to feudalism and to initiate a new historical development of which they were to be the biggest winners (for a while, at least)? While no explicit observations are made in this regard in the debate on the transition from feudalism to capitalism, we do find suggestions that agglomeration, networks and the built environment opened up opportunities for the elite that might have been decisive.

Agglomeration is most often alluded to in the literature. On medieval cities, Reynolds (1997: 155f., 164, 168) writes, "[t]ownsmen form a social unit", and that "geographical propinquity" was its basis. Although this is not peculiarly urban (in rural communities belonging was also negotiated over having one's place there), there were important differences. First, in cities, spatial proximity invited significantly more people to form a collective, which accordingly became larger and hence, at least potentially, more powerful: "Relatively large populations concentrated in relatively small and well-defended areas were thus peculiarly well fitted both to maintain old customs and to develop new ones". Second, in cities, the agglomeration of people meant the massing of actors guided by shared economic interests: "[T]ownspeople had the common interests, the confidence, and the influence to negotiate with their rulers . . . they could do so on whatever subject they wanted, asking for confirmation of their customs, restriction of their dues, or even, if they were ambitious enough, for entirely new privileges". The third difference is, then, that the collectives emerging in cities had a very tangible, material basis, namely accumulation of wealth. Cities' behaviour as "collective seigneur[s]" (Merrington 1975: 178) was buttressed by the claims the people forming these communities could lay on mobile resources, namely money. Merchants operated in networks that, while sometimes covering only the immediate hinterland and sometimes further beyond, always had cities as their central nodes. As a result, money from many places was diverted into these cities. Social concentration and geographical centralization of money went hand-in-hand and gave merchants a lever to move nobles and peasants alike. Usurious interest, for example, according to Marx ([1894] 1991: 937) one of the means through which towns exploited the country, can only be charged where there is enough money in one place – and too little or no money elsewhere.

Reynolds (1997: 165) mentions yet another aspect through which agglomeration has promoted the ability of the townspeople to act jointly. As cities grew and the economic activities conducted in and through them increased, so did the problems – and with them the drive to solve them. Many of the cities' commercial and legal innovations can be interpreted as "responses to the common needs of growing towns" – a notion that corresponds closely with Jacobs' (1997) dictum that cities thrive economically "not because people are smarter in cities, but because of the conditions of density. There is a concentration of need in cities, and a greater incentive to address problems in ways that haven't been addressed before".

Networks are also implied in the debate on the transition from feudalism to capitalism as a source of cities' capability to become the latter's vanguard. The greater the distances over which merchants traded, the more middlemen they had to have at their disposal. Wheat and timber trade with Eastern Europe, for example, had a network of cities from Wismar to Rostock, Danzig, Riga, Tartu and Tallin as its backbone, with the towns often housing sizeable communities of "expats" (German or Dutch merchants) and their accomplices who run the day-to-day businesses. Whereas this control through an inter-city network functioned well for the Hanseatic towns and then for Amsterdam, the bypassing of local merchants and burghers laid the foundations for the re-feudalization and long-lasting peripheralization of Eastern Europe (Van Tielhof 2002).

The built environment – as a source of urban elites' capacity to restructure the relationships with the countryside unevenly – is hardly addressed in the literature on the transition from feudalism to capitalism. Trade, for example, requires fixed infrastructure. Nevertheless, ports and other transport infrastructure are not mentioned separately (scholars seem to take them for granted). However, what is sometimes pointed out is that effective arbitrage (i.e. the exploitation, without risk, of differences in prices at the same time in different places) required storage facilities in the cities, since merchants had to wait until buying- and selling-price differentials became greater. Such storage facilities were also needed for the putting-out system,[16] which spread from around the thirteenth century. Within this system, trade – rather than production – represented the most profitable part of the value chain. Accordingly, it remained monopolized in the hands of the urban merchants, who, however, needed physical infrastructure for this monopolization, namely warehouses where they could store raw materials and finished goods (Dunford & Perrons 1983: 165). Reynolds (1997: 164), finally, points to another aspect that shows how the built environment mattered for the development of towns' unique position: self-governance remained, even if granted, a contested issue, so that those engaged in it usually organized communal assemblies "on defended sites, which generally meant within towns".

The unevenness of the relationships between town and country in the emerging capitalist division of labour, and the proactive role that urban actors played in shaping it, were well understood by the two perhaps most authoritative analysts of capitalism, Adam Smith and Karl Marx. To their analyses we turn in the next section.

---

16. The putting-out system emerged in Flanders and northern Italy and then spread over Western Europe. Formerly independent rural craftsmen became dependent on large merchants engaged in long-distance trade, who provided (credit for) raw materials and sometimes also the means of production to the former craftsmen; in return, these and their families had to produce the required goods at home, for which they received a piece rate.

ADAM SMITH AND KARL MARX: THE SUBJUGATION OF THE COUNTRY TO A CITY-CENTRED DIVISION OF LABOUR

It is well known that understanding how the progressive division of labour during the rise of capitalism contributed to the wealth of nations gave Smith's seminal analysis of capitalism its title ([1776] 1977). This, however, made it imperative for him to address the most fundamental of all divisions of labour, namely that between agriculture and all other economic activities and, accordingly, between the country and the city. In Smith's treatment of this issue we must distinguish two different analytical dimensions. The first refers to what Smith used to call the "natural course of things", that is, the free development of the capitalist market, led only by the famous "invisible hand", while the second took issue with the distortion of this "natural course of things" through establishing monopolies.

Smith, while attributing economic progress to the refinement of the *urban* division of labour (think of his famous example of the pin factory) concedes that ultimately it is agriculture – and hence the country – that is responsible for a nation's development. In a chapter on "the Natural Progress of Opulence" he states that it is the country that

> supplies the town with the means of subsistence and the mater-
> ials of manufacture. . . . The town, in which there neither is nor
> can be any reproduction of substances, may very properly be said
> *to gain its whole wealth and subsistence from the country*. . . . The
> cultivation and improvement of the country, therefore, which
> affords subsistence, must, necessarily, be prior to the increase of
> the town, which furnishes only the means of conveniency and
> luxury. It is the surplus produce of the country *only*, or what is
> over and above the maintenance of the cultivators, that consti-
> tutes the subsistence of the town, which can therefore increase
> only with the increase of this surplus produce. (Smith [1776]
> 1977: 500–502; both emphases added).

For Smith, however, the fact that the country sustains the city does not mean that it is exploited: "We must not . . . imagine that the gain of the town is the loss of the country. The gains of both are mutual and reciprocal, and the division of labour is in this, as in all other cases, advantageous to all the different persons employed in the various occupations into which it is subdivided" ([1776] 1977: 500). Although he acknowledges that for all reci-procity, both sides do not win equally, they nonetheless both win: trade which is "naturally and regularly carried on between any two places is always advantageous, though not always equally so, to both" (*ibid.*: 640). Accordingly, Smith devotes an entire chapter to the question of how "the Commerce of the Towns Contributed to the Improvement of the Country". The reasons are: trade with the city stimulates demand for the country's product, expands cultivation of previously fallow land and leads to productivity growth. The latter because entrepreneurial spirit is injected into the agricultural economy through this trade with the city:

> Merchants . . . are generally the best of all improvers. A merchant is accustomed to employ his money chiefly in profitable projects . . . [because he is used to see] his money go from him and return to him again with a profit . . . [he] is not afraid to lay out at once a large capital upon the improvement of his land when he has a probable prospect of raising the value of it in proportion to the expense. . . . Whoever has had the fortune to live in a mercantile town situated in an unimproved country must have frequently observed how much more spirited the operations of merchants were in this way, than those of mere country gentlemen. (*Ibid.*: 538f.)

Even though Smith frames his analysis of the town–country relationships as a win–win situation, he leaves no doubt as to where the "spirited . . . operations of merchants" were leading. Not necessarily consistent with his claim that the urban–rural relationships were "mutual and reciprocal", but plausible if we take his formulation "improvement of the country" as a euphemism for the capitalization of agriculture and its associated subordination to city-based merchants, Smith notes that "[t]he habits . . . of order, economy, and attention, to which mercantile business naturally forms a merchant, render him much fitter *to execute, with profit and success, any project of improvement* [of the country]" ([1776] 1977: 539; emphasis added). Accordingly, the city and the capital massed there set the conditions for town–country trade: "It is thus that through the greater part of Europe the commerce and manufactures of cities, instead of being the effect, have been the cause and occasion of the improvement and cultivation of the country" (*ibid.*: 549). If we assume with Karl Marx (see below) that not only entrepreneurial spirit is injected into the agricultural economy, but above all profit-hungry capital, then Smith's "improvements" show up as being equal to the subordination of the countryside to the city and the increasing exploitation of rural producers by urban merchants.

Smith, however, by no means left it at the romanticizing notion of "mutual and reciprocal" gains. A proponent of the belief that the free market and competition between economic actors were the best way to achieve "the wealth of nations", he was a vehement opponent of interfering with trade conducted "naturally and regularly". Indeed, Smith was a great enemy of monopolies, which would distort the "natural course of things". While monopolies allowed some actors – Smith frequently points to merchants and manufacturers – to enrich themselves beyond measure, their overall result however, i.e. in national economic terms, would be a slower increase in wealth or even its decrease. Smith's reasoning is as follows: monopolies disrupt the market, making it "constantly understocked", which in turn distorts price formation (because prices of artificially scarce goods would rise "much above the natural price") and artificially increases the profits of the manufacturers producing and of the merchants selling the monopolized items. Two economic damages follow suit: the artificially increased profits would "derange more or less the natural distribution of the stock of the society", i.e. lead to a distortion of the natural arrangement of the production factors, capital and labour. Both are diverted to where the profits are highest, breaking thereby "that natural balance which would otherwise have taken place among all the different branches", as Smith contends with reference to the British industry. Second, artificially high prices for certain goods make them more expensive as inputs for other producers, with the result that the monopoly profits of some come at the expense of the economic dynamism of all. Smith's conclusion for the national economy is unmistakable: "Monopolies . . . are properly established against the very nation which erects them" (Smith [1776] 1977: 91, 837, 800).

For the purpose of this book it is of utmost importance that Smith's reflections on monopolies led him to recognize the possibility of uneven development in urban–rural relationships (Raffer 1987: 13f.). Trade could be exploitative when free price formation is manipulated, through intervention coming from outside the market. According to Smith, the answer to the question of who gains (more) from trade depends on how high wages and profits on either side are. While assuming that a fair equilibrium will develop under free market conditions, Smith admits that such a balance could be disturbed by *political* interventions *in favour of the city*:

> The wages of the workmen, and the profits of their different employers, make up the whole of what is gained upon both. Whatever regulations, therefore, tend to increase those wages and profits beyond what they otherwise would be, tend to enable the town to purchase, with a smaller quantity of its labour, the produce of a greater quantity of the labour of the country. *They give the traders and artificers in the town an advantage over the landlords, farmers, and labourers in the country,* and break down

that natural equality which would otherwise take place in the commerce which is carried on between them. . . . By means of those regulations a greater share of it [the whole annual produce] is given to the inhabitants of the town than would otherwise fall to them; and a less to those of the country. . . . The industry of the town becomes more, and that of the country less advantageous. ([1776] 1977: 177f.; emphasis added)

These "regulations" to which Smith alludes, which "tend to increase . . . wages and profits" above the normal level are primarily monopolies that city-based merchants and manufacturers can obtain by all kinds of means. Referring to seventeenth-century France, Smith describes their attitude as "always demanding [from the government] a monopoly *against* their countrymen", and regarding his own country, he observes that "[t]he government of towns corporate was altogether in the hands of traders and artificers, and it was the manifest interest of every particular class of them to prevent the market from being overstocked, as they commonly express it, with their own particular species of industry, which is in reality to keep it always understocked" ([1776] 1977: 609, 176f.; emphasis added).[17] Overall, uneven development – or, as Smith puts it, "[t]he superiority which the industry of the towns has everywhere in Europe over that of the country" (*ibid.*: 181) – results not from economic ingenuity of urban manufacturers and merchants, but from all kinds of regulations which secure their corporations[18] from competition. The price for this elimination of the market (in the literal sense of higher prices for certain goods, and figuratively as a structural economic disadvantage) is, according to Smith "everywhere finally paid" by the country, namely its "landlords, farmers, and labourers . . . who have seldom opposed the establishment of such monopolies. They have commonly neither inclination nor fitness to enter into combinations; and the clamour and sophistry of merchants and manufacturers easily persuade them that the private interest of a part, and of a subordinate part of the society, is the general interest of the whole" (*ibid.*: 182). Uneven development between cities and the country results: "The inhabitants of a town, though they frequently possess no lands of their own, yet draw to themselves by their industry such a quantity of the rude produce of the lands of other people as supplies them, not only with the materials of their work, but with the fund of their subsistence" (*ibid.*: 901).

---

17. The term "town corporate" refers to self-governing cities endowed with privileges.
18. By being incorporated, Smith means that guilds are formed, the purpose of which was to raise entry barriers and thus limit market access for potential competitors.

Interestingly, Smith applied this notion of uneven development brought about by monopolistic practices not only to the urban–rural relationships, but to "international" trade as well. While he was an advocate of British overseas possessions and of the belief that the control of "foreign" regions and people not only benefited England, but also the colonies and colonized themselves, he saw all these benefits threatened by monopolistic practices of the merchants of his country. He complains that the Navigation Acts[19] "have raised the ordinary rate of British profit higher than it otherwise would have been both in that and in all the other branches of British trade", what disadvantaged the capitals invested in other sectors, induced their flight towards colonial trade and led thereby to a narrowing of Britain's economic activities. Her "commerce, instead of running in a great number of small channels, has been taught to run principally in one great channel. But the whole system of her industry and commerce has thereby been rendered less secure, the whole state of her body politic less healthful than it otherwise would have been". Accordingly, while the monopoly augmented "the gain of our merchants", it also "obstructs the natural increase of capital, it tends rather to diminish than to increase the sum total of the revenue which the inhabitants of the country derive from the profits of stock. . . . The monopoly raises the rate of profit, but it hinders the sum of profit from rising so high as it otherwise would do". In sum, therefore, "[i]f the colony trade . . . is advantageous to Great Britain, it is not by means of the monopoly, but in spite of the monopoly" (Smith [1776] 1977: 792, 800, 810f., 806).

Remarkably, Smith criticized not only that "the interest of the mother country was sacrificed" to "the interest of those merchants", but also that of the colonies. While the companies that engage in colonial trade under the protection of a monopoly that obliges the colonized population to buy all European goods from them, and to sell to them all their own goods, would make "exorbitant and oppressive" profits, the colonies themselves would remain "ill supplied" and obliged "both to buy very dear, and to sell very cheap". This, Smith concludes, "keeps down the revenue of the inhabitants of that country below what it would naturally rise to, and thereby diminishes their power of accumulation. It not only hinders, at all times, their capital from maintaining so great a quantity of productive labour as it would otherwise maintain, but it hinders it from increasing so fast as it would otherwise increase". And elsewhere he states that treaties that colonies conclude and that grant monopoly rights to British (and other colonizers') companies,

---

19. The Navigation Acts are a series of laws from 1651 onwards which restricted trade between England and the colonies to English ships.

"though they may be advantageous to the merchants and manufacturers of the favoured, are necessarily disadvantageous to those of the favouring country. A monopoly is thus granted *against them* to a foreign nation". Smith offers, however, some consolation to his British readers: while the monopoly of the colony trade depresses the industry of all countries, it does so "chiefly [with] that of the colonies". For Britain, on the other hand, it is true that "[t]he natural good effects of the colony trade . . . more than counterbalance . . . the bad effects of the monopoly, so that, monopoly and all together, that trade . . . is not only advantageous, but greatly advantageous". Against this backdrop, he concedes that the "maintenance of this monopoly has hitherto been the principal, or more properly perhaps the sole end and purpose of the dominion which Great Britain assumes over her colonies" (Smith [1776] [1776] 1977: 771, 760, 806, 715, 809, 814; emphasis added).

Raffer (1987: 14) points out that Smith's assessments of the adverse effects of monopoly in trade and production resemble theories of unequal exchange developed almost 200 years later by Arghiri Emmanuel, Samir Amin and others. Replace "town" by "North" or "First World" and "country" by "South" or "Third World", and Smith's notion "is Emmanuel's model put into a nutshell". And just like the later dependency theorists, Smith had a keen sense of the geographic dimensions of this inequality, i.e. of the issue of the urban–rural and the "North–South" divide, and also of the role played by the city in the context of monopolies and uneven development. We have already seen that he attributed cities' economic superiority less to the merchants' and manufacturers' genius, but to all kinds of regulations that protected them from competition. Smith saw very clearly that the economic vitality that the European medieval cities were to acquire was initially induced from the outside: "The privileges which we find granted by ancient charters to the inhabitants of some of the principal towns in Europe sufficiently show what they were before those grants. . . . They seem, indeed, to have been a very poor, mean set of people, who used to travel about with their goods from place to place, and from fair to fair, like the hawkers and pedlars of the present times" (Smith [1776] 1977: 523).

Smith was also well aware of the uneven development induced thereby: privileging cities and freeing their economic activities from competition increased "the rate of mercantile and manufacturing profit *in proportion to that of agricultural profit*", which had a negative impact on the accumulation dynamics of the latter: A monopoly for urban activities

> either draws from agriculture a part of the capital which had before been employed in it, or hinders from going to it a part of what would otherwise have gone to it. . . . Agriculture is rendered

less advantageous, and trade and manufactures more advantageous than they otherwise would be; and every man [sic] is tempted by his own interest to turn, as much as he can, both his capital and his industry from the former to the latter employments. ([1776] 1977: 893f.; emphasis added)

However, Smith also mentions that the cities' economic success was not only based on monopolistic practices (which he despised as unfair), but also on their particular political-military position: cities enjoyed, thanks to their self-government and their walls, security against the arbitrariness of the various feudal lords – an important push for investment readiness. But that was not all: once the feudal authorities had created "places [which] were set apart and defended by laws or privileges making them market and production centres" (Hibbert 1965: 197), cities were also promoted and favoured in the further course of history. The political economy of the forming nation states in Europe, Smith ([1776] 1977: 904) complains, has been, via various regulatory interventions into the market, "more favourable to manufactures and foreign trade, the industry of the towns, than to agriculture, the industry of the country".

It is no wonder, then, that Smith implicitly and also explicitly associates "monopoly" with "town" again and again. Interestingly, he did so not only because the medieval city was born as a certain monopoly, and because monopoly-hungry merchants and manufacturers were city-based, but also because he was aware of the exceptional conditions that the city itself offered some of its actors to pursue such monopolies and to prosper economically at the expense of others. Smith provides some evidence that merchants and manufacturers succeeded in acquiring monopoly positions on the basis of typical urban characteristics, namely agglomeration and networks. He notes that inhabitants of a town have, *because of their physical proximity*, the opportunity to collude against rural producers. Unlike them, who live further apart and who therefore "cannot easily combine together", the inhabitants of a town,

being collected into one place, can easily combine together. The most insignificant trades carried on in towns have accordingly, in some place or other, been incorporated, and even where they have never been incorporated, yet the corporation spirit, the jealousy of strangers, the aversion to take apprentices, or to communicate the secret of their trade, generally prevail in them, and often teach them, by voluntary associations and agreements, *to prevent that free competition* which they cannot prohibit by bye-laws. (Smith [1776] 1977: 179; emphasis added)

In several places Smith links the enforcement of monopolies to the opportunities created by the conditions of the city which allow for coordinating strategies in order to act consistently vis-à-vis the individual (because isolated) rural producer, and to circumvent the market. In his attacks against monopolies, he attributes their "wretched spirit" to the *urban* "undertaker[s]", particularly to

> merchants and manufacturers, who, *being collected into towns*, and accustomed to that *exclusive corporation spirit which prevails in them*, naturally endeavour to obtain against all their countrymen the same exclusive privilege which they generally possess against the inhabitants of their respective towns. They accordingly seem to have been the original inventors of those restraints upon the importation of foreign goods which secure to them the monopoly of the home market (Smith ([1776] 1977: 602; both emphases added).

A further relevant aspect of agglomeration is that it facilitated the overlap and even fusion of political authority with economic power – what Arrighi (1994: 12) has called the transition from "scattered to concentrated capitalist power" and assessed as the "really important transition that needs to be elucidated" (see first section in this chapter). Smith observes that the "government of towns corporate was altogether in the hands of traders and artificers" and that this takeover of political power allowed them to "establish regulations proper for this purpose [the enforcement of monopolies]" (Smith [1776] 1977: 176f.). He gives a very practical example from everyday economic life, namely the obligation of people of the same trade "to enter their names and places of abode in a public register", what then "facilitates" their coming together. This law, Smith criticizes, "connects individuals who might never otherwise be known to one another, and gives every man [sic] of the trade a direction where to find every other man of it" (*ibid.*: 183). The result of such assemblies then is, that "the conversation ends in a conspiracy against the public, or in some contrivance to raise prices".

Smith also mentions, albeit less extensively, advantages arising for city-based actors from the other two dimensions of typical urban properties, namely networks and the built environment. Cities are nodes of transport routes, and this gives merchants access to markets beyond their immediate vicinity. A resulting advantage is the facilitation of market expansion and the associated increase of own production. London and Calcutta, Smith notes, "carry on a very considerable commerce with each other, and by mutually affording a market, give a good deal of encouragement to each other's industry" ([1776] 1977: 37). Moreover, innovations also reach the city through the networks that connect them to other cities – "foreign commerce of some of their [the states of Europe] cities has introduced all their finer manufactures", Smith (*ibid*.: 506) observes. While we re-encounter such notions in today's literature on inter-city networks (think, for example, of Jacobs' idea of import replacements; see Chapter 3), Smith adds a third advantage that cities derive from their embeddedness in networks, which is rarely found in today's debates but is key to uneven development. He argues that due to inter-city networks, merchants enjoy a kind of "reverse" monopoly – a monopsony, in which many sellers face only one buyer. And he sharpens this notion to urban–rural relations. Cities, contends Smith,

> situated near either the sea coast or the banks of a navigable river, are not necessarily confined to derive them [food and inputs for the city's industry] from the country in their neighbourhood. They have a much wider range, and may draw them from the most remote corners of the world . . . A city might in this manner grow up to great wealth and splendour, while not only the country in its neighbourhood, but all those to which it traded, were in poverty and wretchedness. (*ibid*.: 531f.)

The "much wider range" that access to inter-city networks gives merchants translates into the option to choose between different rural suppliers for the goods they wish to purchase because each city in the network offers access to its own hinterland. Rural producers, however, generally depend, isolated as they are, on just *one* urban market. The result is that once again reciprocal trade (which, according to Smith, would be the natural course of things) is turned into an uneven one.

References to the role of the built environment are scarce but can be found. First of all, Smith mentions that the physical fortification of cities, like self-government, offered protection from feudal lords and was therefore an incentive to invest. As to his discussion of monopolies' role in engendering uneven development, Smith mentions the possibility of establishing an "exclusive company" by forcing the whole commerce with the colonies through a "a particular port of the mother country". This geographical concentration of trade made strict control possible – "no ship was allowed to sail, but either in a fleet and at a particular season, or, if single, in consequence of a particular licence, which in most cases was very well paid for" ([1776] 1977: 760). Beyond its immediate practical function, the built environment thus served to make other regulations governable and enforceable. The result was similar to the trade of the "exclusive companies": While theoretically this policy opened "the trade of the colonies to all the natives of the mother country, provided they traded from the proper port, at the proper season, and in the proper vessels", what happened de facto was that

> all the different merchants, who joined their stocks in order to fit out those licensed vessels, would find it for their interest to act in concert, [for which reason] the trade which was carried on in this manner would necessarily be conducted very nearly upon the same principles as that of an exclusive company. The profit of those merchants would be almost equally exorbitant and oppressive. The colonies would be ill supplied, and would be obliged both to buy very dear, and to sell very cheap. (*ibid.*)

Just as for Adam Smith, reflecting on the division of labour was the starting point for Karl Marx's engagement with the relationships between town and country. "The greatest division of material and mental labour is the separation of town and country", wrote Marx and Engels ([1845–46] 1974: 68f.), which accordingly is "[t]he foundation of every division of labour which has attained a certain degree of development" (Marx [1890] 1976: 472). Consequently, the seperation of town and country is the prerequisite of any economic development.

Two specifications are appropriate. According to Marx's conviction that the central organizing element of any society is the mode of production, the *geographical* division of labour between town and country, although fundamental and an historical constant across societies, is not considered to be a distinct analytical category. Rather, it is an expression of the prevailing form of the *social* division of labour and its imperatives, which in turn follow from the mode of production. The city, and for that matter its relationships to rural environments, does therefore not assume the rank of a fundamental concept in Marx's analysis of the rural–urban dichotomy. Nevertheless, and not necessarily consistent with the first point, Marx describes the town–country relationships *in principle* – that is, for every mode of production so far, not just the capitalist one – as not being in mutual interest, but rather as conflictual and polarizing. In *Capital*, Marx ([1890] 1976: 472, both emphasis added) notes "that the *whole economic history* of society is summed up in the movement of this *antithesis*" between city and country, while in *German Ideology* he and Engels write that the "division of labour inside a nation leads . . . to the separation of *town* and *country* and to the *conflict of their interests*", with "[t]he *antagonism* between town and country . . . [running] through *the whole history of civilisation* to the present day" (Marx & Engels [1845–46] 1974: 43, 69, second, third and fourth emphases added). For the Middle Ages, for example, whose mode of production was country-based,

Marx nevertheless contends that "the town everywhere and without exception exploited the countryside economically through its monopoly prices, its taxation system, its guilds, its direct commercial trickery and its usury" ([1894] 1991: 937).

So, while Marx asserts that in every mode of production the relationships between city and country were different, he nevertheless assumes a generic character of this relation as uneven, leading to an epoch-spanning urban–rural dichotomy. While the latter is quite plausible, since urbanization has always involved the production, appropriation, geographical transfer and use of agricultural surpluses, Marx and Engels nevertheless stuck to maintaining that the city has no independent standing within the division of labour (Katznelson 1994).

With the implementation of the capitalist mode of production, the social division of labour and hence the relationships between town and country fundamentally changed. And so too did cities. "I accept the [Marxian] idea", writes David Harvey (1985: 1), whose *Urbanization of Capital* is still the authoritative Marxist analysis of the city, "that the 'urban' has a specific meaning under the capitalist mode of production". Cities, then, are not just cities in a capitalist world, but rather they are *capitalist cities*. Accordingly, in the *Grundrisse* (Marx [1857–61] 1973: 108), in which Marx outlines his analysis of the capitalist mode of production, "[t]own and country" are mentioned, immediately after "[c]apital, wage labour, landed property" as fundamental categories "which make up the inner structure of bourgeois society and on which the fundamental classes rest". A key difference from pre-capitalist times is that they occupy a much more dominant position in the economy and in society, which has also intensified the traditional conflict of interests ("antithesis") between town and country: with the imposition of the capitalist mode of production, it takes on the character of "ruthless terrorism" (Marx [1890] 1976: 895) on the part of the city. Cities for the first time in history gained the upper hand:

The history of classical antiquity is the history of cities, but of cities founded on landed property and on agriculture; Asiatic history is a kind of indifferent unity of town and countryside (the really large cities must be regarded here merely as royal camps, as works of artifice . . . erected over the economic construction proper); the Middle Ages (Germanic period) begins with the land as the seat of history, whose further development then moves forward in the contradiction between town and countryside; the modern [age] is the urbanization of the countryside, not ruralization of the city as in antiquity. (Marx [1857–61] 1973: 479)

While this oft-quoted paragraph shows Marx's conviction that the city and urban-based actors gradually have become the centre of gravity of human history, it nevertheless does not do justice to the meaning of the original due to poor translation. The German original reads: "*die moderne [Geschichte] ist Verstädtischung des Landes, nicht wie bei den Antiken Verländlichung der Stadt*" (Marx [1857–61] 1983: 391). "*Verstädtischung*" is a German word no longer in use today, but that was formerly used analogously to "*Verstaatlichung*" (nationalization) (DWDS 2022). This linguistic detail is important because it shows that "urbanization of the countryside" is a misleading translation that obscures what Marx presumably wanted to say. Just as nationalization means bringing something (land, an industry, etc.,) under state ownership or control, "*Verstädtischung*" means bringing something *under the control of cities*. Accordingly, the decisive change that the advent of the capitalist mode of production brought about was not the urbanization of the countryside as it is commonly thought (more densely populated, infrastructure, modern manners, etc.), but that it came under the control of cities. Even though Marx, in his analysis of the geography of the imposition of the capitalist mode of production in England, does not go beyond a national economic perspective and does not directly address the city, it is clear that for him the cradle of capitalism was there: "The separation of town and country", he and Engels write ([1845–46] 1974: 69), "can also be understood as the separation of capital and landed property, as the beginning of the existence and development of capital independent of landed property – the beginning of property having its basis only in labour and exchange". It is in the city where the "*formation of money-wealth*" (Marx [1857–61] 1973: 509; emphasis in original) by merchants took place, which Marx, on the one hand, attributes to the "prehistory" (*ibid.*), but of which, on the other hand, he says that it "was from the beginning movable, capital in the modern sense as far as one can speak of it, given the circumstances of those times" (Marx & Engels [1845–46] 1974: 73). And Marx ([1890] 1976: 876), like many scholars after him, points to "certain towns of the Mediterranean", where "we come across the first sporadic traces of capitalist production as early as the fourteenth or fifteenth centuries".[20]

Capital as a social relation is thus of urban origin, and the *Verstädtischung des Landes*, the bringing of rural producers under the control of the city

---

20. However, Marx also emphasizes that the cities, in the course of the development from handicraft to manufacture to industry, became the brakes on capitalism because the medieval city with its guild system was too restrictive for the development of the productive forces.

and its actors, is part of this process. "*Verstädtischung des Landes*" means that a clear hierarchy – in terms of a chain of command – was established between the city and the country. In the *Communist Manifesto* Marx and Engels ([1890] 1955: 14; all emphases added) describe this as follows: "The bourgeoisie has *subjected the country to the rule of the towns*. It has created enormous cities, has greatly increased the urban population as compared with the rural, and has thus rescued a considerable part of the population from the idiocy of rural life. [. . .] it has made *the country dependent on the towns*". This subjugating of the country and its producers took place in the course of the original accumulation, a process through which capital came to be. Rural producers were divorced from their means of production and subsistence, essentially through direct violence and legal regulations accompanying and supporting it. By "freeing" the former tenants, farmers and rural craftsmen, the widespread expropriation created the mass of those who were to sell their labour in the urban factories, and by making agricultural production more dynamic, it created the surplus of food that fed (albeit poorly) the new industrial workers. The money-wealth already mentioned, which merchants had amassed in cities, were a central means in this "process of divorce", because it "could place itself as mediator between the objective conditions of life, thus liberated, and the liberated but also *homeless* and *emptyhanded* labour powers, and buy the latter with the former" (Marx [1857–61] 1973: 509; emphasis in original).

In *Capital*, Marx, without using the term, describes the "*Verstädtischung des Landes*" in the course of the original accumulation as simultaneous modernization and degradation. In the now "capitalist agriculture"

[i]n spite of the smaller number of its cultivators, the soil brought forth as much produce as before, or even more, because the revolution in property relations on the land was accompanied by improved methods of cultivation, greater co-operation, a higher concentration of the means of production and so on, and because the agricultural wage labourers were made to work at a higher level of intensity, and the field of production on which they worked for themselves shrank more and more. With the 'setting free' of a part of the agricultural population, therefore, their former means of nourishment were also set free. They were now transformed into material elements of variable capital. The peasant, expropriated and cast adrift, had to obtain the value of the means of subsistence from his new lord, the industrial capitalist, in the form of wages. And the same thing happened to those raw materials of industry which depended on indigenous

agriculture. They were transformed into an element of constant capital. (Marx [1890] 1976: 895, 908f.)

However, as economic space, the countryside became the cities' hinterland (literally, the land "behind"), without production in its own right, since the expropriation of the peasants and their separation from their own means of production "goes hand in hand" with "the destruction of the subsidiary trades of the countryside, the process whereby manufacture is divorced from agriculture". This elimination "of the subsidiary trades of the countryside" was as necessary for the triumph of capitalism as the expropriation of the peasants, because "only the destruction of rural domestic industry can give the home market of a country that extension and stability which the capitalist mode of production requires" (Marx [1890] 1976: 911). But that's not all: the "*Verstädtischung des Landes*" ultimately leads to its complete destruction because "all progress in capitalist agriculture is a progress in the art, not only of robbing the worker, but of robbing the soil; all progress in increasing the fertility of the soil for a given time is a progress towards ruining the more longlasting sources of that fertility" (*ibid.*: 638).

Of course, the new urban–rural hierarchy was not enforced by the cities as such, but by actors within them, namely the bourgeoisie. This is, however, "*inherently urban*", as Peter Taylor (2013: 56; emphasis added) affirms. While the word comes from the French and originally referred to the citizenry or freemen of a town, in Marxist terminology, "bourgeoisie" refers to the class of those privately owning the means of production. What is crucial for the "inherently urban" being of the bourgeoisie is that the city offered opportunities to attain such a dominant position. There are numerous (albeit scattered and unsystematized) references to this circumstance in the work of Marx and Engels, and it is not without reason that in the previously quoted passage in the *Communist Manifesto* they not only say in general terms that the bourgeoisie has subjugated the country, but also specify to whom, namely to the "rule of the towns". Therefore, the country became dependent not in the abstract, but rather specifically "on the towns" (Marx & Engels [1890] 1955: 14). Although it is not stated explicitly, the quote nevertheless indicates that the city is identified with the bourgeoisie. While this does not necessarily imply that cities and their networks were a requirement for the capitalist mode of production to take hold, it does suggest that the city is a theoretically specific object for the analysis of the rise of capitalism.

Of the three factors underlying the genius of cities – agglomeration, intercity networks, built environment – it is the first, in particular, that recurs again and again in the writings of Marx and Engels as having been central to the rise of the bourgeoisie and to the imposition of the capitalist mode of production. Marx suggests in the *Grundrisse* that the specific density resulting from the concentration of capitalists, money, labour, machines, and so on, in the city makes a difference to social action. He distinguishes between the mere coming-together (*Vereinigung*) of economic actors, and their "being-together . . . as a unity". Only the latter leads to the formation of a *Verein* (community), which is characterized by the fact that its economic actors are capable of acting in concert (and not as a sum of independent subjects), comparable to a state or political body: "the commune [*Gemeinde*] possesses an economic existence as such; the city's mere *presence*, as such, distinguishes it from a mere multiplicity of independent houses. The whole, here, consists not merely of its parts. It is a kind of independent organism" ([1857–61] 1973: 483; emphasis in original). Quite consistent with Merrington's (1975: 178) later formulation of the medieval city as a "'collective seigneur'", Marx and Engels in *The German Ideology*, refer to the city as an "organised community" that gained agency because of the self-organization of its owning citizens: "These towns were true 'associations', called forth by the direct need, the care of providing for the protection of property, and of multiplying the means of production and defiance of the separate members" ([1845–46] 1974: 70). One result of this bringing together of individual interests into a common denominator was to shape the law, which is a state (or, as in nothern Italy) city-state matter, according to merchants' own interests: "The very first town which carried on an extensive maritime trade in the Middle Ages, Amalfi, also developed maritime law" (*ibid*.: 80).

In addition to its contribution to the formation of a social unity of the owners of capital, agglomeration was functional in other respects for the enforcement of the capitalist mode of production. As already indicated, the money gathered and controlled by city-based merchants operating within inter-city networks was indispensable for the original accumulation. Although for Marx these merchants were not capitalist actors in the true sense of the word (because their profits stemmed not from exploiting labour, but from arbitrage), they nevertheless were originators of capital. Merchants' profit-making laid the foundation for the formation of capital, because it centralized mobile and dispersed money, which, until then, had been floating around in small and micro quantities. This centralization was a social as well a geographical process – money became concentrated in the hands of a few, and in the cities where these few operated. Through this bringing together – *agglomeration* – of money, an instrument was created that could be used to produce more money. Capital, writes Marx, necessarily "begins with *money* and hence with wealth existing in the form of money" ([1857–61] 1973: 505; emphasis in original).

The social concentration and the geographical centralization of money were not only indispensable for the amounts needed for the separation of rural producers from their means of production. It was also necessary for the emergence of capital proper (i.e. industrial capital). Sufficient money for investment was available only in (certain) cities, namely those into which the merchants – the cities' elite at that time – channelled the money they siphoned from producers and merchants in the rural areas and smaller towns. In this sense, Marx causally links the social and the spatial reorganization of production, both as preconditions for the enforcement of the capitalist mode of production. Although he saw the purely economic benefits resulting from a deepened division of labour and the agglomeration of economic activities and workers, namely the development of economies of scale and an increase in productivity, he went far beyond this notion. Marx emphasized that the geographical centralization of the means of production as well as of labour were indispensable for the concentration of property and therefore for the capitalist mode of production to prevail. In the *Communist Manifesto*, he and Engels point to this connection quite clearly: "More and more the bourgeoisie keeps doing away with the scattered state of the population, of the means of production, and of property. It has agglomerated population, centralized means of production, and has concentrated property in a few hands" (Marx & Engels [1890] 1955: 14, emphasis added). And in *Capital*, Marx writes:

> Capitalist production only really begins . . . when each individual capital simultaneously employs a comparatively large number of workers, and when, as a result, the labour process is carried on an extensive scale, and yields relatively large quantities of products. A large number of workers working together, at the same time, *in one place* . . . in order to produce the same sort of commodity under the command of the same capitalist, constitutes the starting point of capitalist production. This is true both historically and conceptually. ([1890] 1976: 439; emphasis added)

The transformation of the labour process into a social one (a prerequisite for the capitalist mode of production) required that labour (workers), the means of production (machinery) and control over them (capitalists) were centralized in space, namely in cities. Only through the agglomeration of workers "in one place", in order "to produce the same sort of commodity" and "under the command of the same capitalist", workers "ceased to belong to themselves" and "are incorporated into capital" (Marx ([1890] 1976: 439, 449).

We also find references in Marx to the importance of inter-city networks for the enforcement of the capitalist mode of production, albeit relatively few and not systematized. One aspect he mentions is that inter-city networks were functional to the development of the productive forces because technological and labour-organizational developments spread through inter-city trade. "The towns enter into relations *with one another*", whereby the "local restrictions of earlier times [of tools and the state of division of labour] begin gradually to be broken down" (Marx & Engels [1845–46] 1974: 72; emphasis in original). In its place, a standard of production is created that transcends local space – the socially necessary labour time to produce a commodity. Yet, this new standard, imposed equally on all production and all producers, not only transcends local space, it is decidedly urban. As the measure of the value of a commodity, the socially necessary labour time, together with the related concept of the average rate of profit, is at the heart of Marx's theory – and both are urban phenomena: "The average profit and the price of production governed by it are formed *outside the rural situation, in the orbit of urban trade and manufacture*" (Marx [1894] 1991: 936; emphasis added).

However, Marx ascribes another, namely political, significance to inter-city networks. If agglomeration is a necessary condition for the development of class consciousness among the wealthy citizens, then connections between cities across space are equally important. "In the Middle Ages", Marx and Engels write,

> the burghers in every city were forced to unite against the nobility to defend themselves; the expansion of trade, the establishment of communications led the individual cities to get to know other cities that had asserted the same interests in the struggle with the same opposition. From the many local citizenships of the individual cities, the bourgeois class emerged only very gradually.... *With the occurrence of the connection between the individual cities, these common conditions [the living conditions of the individual burghers] developed into class conditions. The* same conditions, the same opposition, the same interests had to produce, on the whole, the same customs everywhere. The bourgeoisie itself develops only gradually with its conditions.[21] ([1845–46] 1978: 53; emphasis added)

In sum, even though under the capitalist mode of production both industrial and agricultural workers are all under the real domination of capital,

---

21. This sentence is missing in the English translation of the *Deutsche Ideologie*. Translation by the author and quoted according to the German edition.

the urban–rural contrast does not lose its importance. As a social relation (and not a "thing" that is easily made local), capitalism develops in and through geography. The spaces of capitalist control and exploitation span across places, connecting them unevenly. The city, where the material bases of the capitalist relationships (e.g. money, machines) are as centralized as the social ones (capitalists, workers), has a special role to play. To be sure, capitalism neither invented the city nor the agglomeration economies and network externalities it generates; it found them, took possession of them, transformed them, and used them. What is decisive, however, is that the emergence of capitalism required a specific spatial form, namely agglomeration, the geographical centralization of both constant and variable capital, as Marx pointed out. Accordingly, capitalism not only has to urbanize in order to *reproduce* itself, as David Harvey (1985: 222) said, it came into existence through cities' essential features.

In the next section I shall present Fernand Braudel's interpretation of cities as "aggressive world[s]" (1984: 94) – for me the most important source of inspiration for my thinking about the Janus-facedness of the genius of cities. As Braudel deals with the rise and expansion of capitalism from the fifteenth to the eighteenth centuries, the geographical perspective widens to include not only cities in northwestern Europe and Italy, but also in the newly emerged peripheries in America and in Eastern Europe, as well as in China and India.

CITIES AS AGGRESSIVE WORLDS: FERNAND BRAUDEL'S UNDERSTANDING OF A CITY-DRIVEN CAPITALISM

Probably more than any other scholar, Fernand Braudel examined history through the lens of cities: "Interpreted properly, their study leads to a general and unusually comprehensive view of the whole history of material life", he wrote (Braudel 1985: 556). This is also true for his analysis of the rise and functioning of capitalism, in which the city is perhaps the most essential analytical instrument. There are two reasons for the importance Braudel attached to cities. First, he had a genuine interest in geography. Braudel's life project *geohistoire* conceptualizes space as a central factor in the development of societies, but without becoming deterministic. Rather, physical geography – rivers and mountains, plains and seas, climate, soil and vegetation – provides conditions upon which people act. Therefore, space is not just a natural given – by using it and acting through it, people produce and transform geographies. In this way, Braudel's *geohistoire* becomes an analysis that brings geography and history together as equally important dimensions of social life. Secondly, Braudel's understanding of capitalism focused on trade, and on long-distance trade in particular: "The pre-conditions of any form of capitalism have to do with circulation. . . . The wider circulation stretched its net, the more profitable it was. . . . long distance trade . . . [was] an essential factor in the creation of merchant capitalism" (Braudel 1983: 582, 408).

Taken together, *"geohistoire"* and "merchant capitalism" put cities centre stage. While the former raised questions about the "where?" and the "why there?", the latter sparked interest for trade routes and their nodal points. "Cities and their communications, communications and their cities" – for Braudel (1972: 277) this is the basis of all human-made geography, at least since the reawakening of long-distance trade and the resurgence of cities in the High Middle Ages. Indeed, he is an admirer of cities' virtuosity. Cities are, Braudel writes (1985: 479; 1984: 312), "turning-points, watersheds of human history", "indispensable to the general process of growth", and this because of the extraordinary dynamics they are capable of igniting: "Towns are like electric transformers. They increase the tension, accelerate the rhythms of exchange, and constantly recharge human life" (Braudel 1985: 479).

For Braudel, cities were always and everywhere extraordinarily dynamic, and they are therefore also the birthplaces of capitalism, the "essential instruments of accumulation . . . everything came from the towns, everything started there" (1984: 311f.). For periods when few historians speak of capitalism, Braudel (*ibid.*: 105) identifies it in the commercial practices of Hanseatic towns which "clung to an elementary kind of capitalism", whereas Florence of the fourteenth century was considered "an early home of capitalism" (Braudel 1983: 563). Accordingly, "[c]apitalism and towns were basically the same thing in the West" (Braudel 1985: 514). This equation runs through Braudel's work, and it applies in both directions: not only did capitalism have its "home" in cities, it is *genuinely urban*, originating not only in, but *from* cities, namely those in Western Europe, in a corridor of cities roughly corresponding to what is today known as the "Blue Banana" or the Liverpool–Milan axis. Braudel's equation of capitalism with cities applies not only for the big metropolis: regarding Varzy, for example, a small French town that today has little more than 1,000 inhabitants, he notes that it "was well and truly a town, with its own bourgeoisie" (which is, as we know, the standard bearer of capitalism). And he adds: "There are thousands of similar examples" (*ibid.*: 482). And, another case of equating cities with capitalism, this time with reference to Western Europe as a whole: "This favoured part of Europe was too available for exploitation by cities, bourgeoisies, rich merchants or enterprising nobles" (Braudel 1983: 280). As to capitalism as a world-spanning system, Braudel (1984: 25–7) contends that it is one of the "ground rules" that a "world-economy always has an urban centre of gravity, a city, as the logistic heart of its activity". But a single, individual city does not. Capitalism needs cities in the plural, it develops out of them, the dominating city at its centre is necessarily sustained by extensive inter-city networks. So it is part of Braudel's ground rule that there must be other towns, which support, in a subordinate relationship, the central city.

Braudel's work is so important to the idea of the Janus-faced genius of cities because, however much he admires towns' vitality, he is not blinded by it. For Braudel (1984: 94, 311f., 35), cities are "aggressive world[s]" *in two senses*: they are forceful, potent and energetic, "indispensable to the general process of growth", but they also provide the social and physical environments that allow elites to forge "weapons of domination" which are necessary to subjugate and exploit others. Cities belong to the structures of capitalism not only because they drive innovation and growth, but also because, as "essential instruments of accumulation", they are "an active force for unequal exchange". Braudel arrives at this conclusion on the basis of two insights: capitalism is always about growth *and* exploitation and polarization, and exploitation and polarization always have social *and* spatial dimensions. Accordingly, the growth that cities produce cannot be separated from uneven development. The capitalist world economy is "marked by a hierarchy: the area is always a sum of individual economies, some poor, some modest, with a comparatively rich one in the centre. As a result, there are *inequalities, differences of voltage which make possible the functioning of the whole*" (Braudel 1984: 26; emphasis added). As central organs of capitalism, cities and their networks are impregnated with this inequality. According to Braudel (1985: 481, 557), cities by definition live off asymmetrical relationships: "The town only exists as a town in relation to a form of life lower than its own". Cities "do not arise of their own volition . . . [they arise] because capital and surplus wealth is poured into them". Merchants – for Braudel the most important capitalist actors of the time – needed, if they wanted to prosper, a city's catchment area, "larger states to batten on" (Braudel 1984: 91).

Like Smith, Marx and many others, Braudel sees the division of labour between agriculture and all other activities as one of the most fundamental structures of economic activity (not only in capitalism) and as the foundation upon which cities could arise. What distinguishes Braudel's work, however, is that it offers a truly citified analysis of the workings of this division of labour, and thereby also of the social and spatial inequalities produced and maintained by it. Although he never explicitly elaborated a theory of cities, Braudel's citified analysis of the rise of capitalism brings him to make two points more clearly than other scholars. First, the urban–rural division of labour not only worked in favour of the city, but it was intention-ally created by urban actors in such a way that towns could "channel . . . to their own advantage" any growth achieved. Accordingly, "the exchange economy . . . operated on behalf of the towns and led to the towns" (Braudel 1985: 479, 356f.). Second, urban elites could shape the division of labour in their own and in their cities' favour because they had at their disposal cities' "supply architecture" (Storper 2013: 9). All three dimensions of cities' genius discussed above – agglomeration economies, external networks, and a massive built environment – figure prominently in Braudel's account of cities' role in the rise of capitalism *and* in the associated socio-spatial polar-ization. For Braudel, cities are enabling environments for "good" as well as for "bad" innovations, because of the externalities that arise from the urban properties named.

In the High Middle Ages, Europe experienced a remarkable demographic and economic development, and cities and their networks grew in number, size and density. Both developments were interconnected, and for Braudel it is quite clear that the second promoted the first. Crucial in the context of this book, he points out that cities achieved this by restructuring divisions of labour: "A clear distinction of functions, a 'division of labour' between town and countryside, sometimes brutally felt, became the norm". So antagonistic was the enforced relationship that Braudel (1985: 484; 1984: 312) speaks of a "version of the class struggle" between towns and country and of cities as "semiparasitical systems". The notion of "parasitic" cities stems from Bernd Hoselitz (1955; see next section), who developed it to denote colonial capital cities that siphoned off the surplus of the country for (luxury) consumption, without providing any "development" at the origin of the surplus. Braudel, who does not refer to Hoselitz, speaks of semiparasitic cities because, according to him, while cities enrich themselves, they also multiply the wealth they appropriate and partially redistribute it into a "national" economy.

What is the basis for these harsh assessments? As the passage quoted above, according to which Braudel sees in cities "an active force for unequal exchange" already suggests, the urban–rural relationship is for Braudel a specific scale in capitalist development which depends on "differences in voltage" (Braudel 1985: 441, 510) and which therefore is inevitably uneven. The urban–rural relationship "is a good example . . . of unequal exchange. . . . it has clearly been a force to be reckoned with from early on". Towns "ruled their countrysides autocratically, regarding them exactly as later powers regarded their colonies, and treating them as such".

The capitalist division of labour that was established consisted of different zones, namely a core – quite small –, a middle zone and a periphery, the largest of the three. How did cores and peripheries come into existence? How did cities maintain the "poor regions on their doorsteps . . . deliberately or not, in their poverty" (Braudel 1972: 386)? The basic rule was to concentrate on the profitable activities and to leave the less profitable or even non-profitable ones to others or to impose them on them. Among the profitable activities was first and foremost trade (and, in particular, long-distance trade), money markets (especially lending) and certain craft (or early industrial) activities, namely those requiring particular skills. However, some agricultural production could also be included, as we shall see in a moment. Unprofitable activities were primarily associated with the production of staple foods such as wheat and other grains, but also of timber, and those craft or industrial activities that required less skill.

The epitome of such a profit-structured division of labour was Venice, whose activities all fell, because of its location, into the non-agricultural. Critically, however, the city made a virtue out of necessity – focusing on industry, commerce and other services was quite appropriate because "labour was more profitably employed [there] than in rural activities" (Braudel 1984: 108). Other cities adopted this model of a division of labour structured according to opportunities for profit. Florence, for example, was rich in farmland, but its elites found it more lucrative to grow vines and olives in the immediate hinterland and to import grain from Sicily. And Amsterdam, surrounded by fertile land, also supplied itself from far away: from the Baltic wheat and rye, from Denmark meat and from the North Sea herrings. In these, and many other cases, it was true that the powerful city avoided carrying the heavy burden of the primary sector. Urban elites sought to leave "all the ungrateful tasks, the deliveries of raw materials" (Braudel 1983: 570) to people in the countryside. There, accordingly, only those activities remained which "the towns were glad enough to leave to them" (Braudel 1985: 488).

The relationship between profitable and non-profitable activities and hence between cities and the countryside can be further illustrated by the example of the wheat trade. When it was marketed locally, it involved many middlemen so that "[t]here was little or no profit accumulation here . . . Most of the profit . . . went to the transporters who were the real beneficiaries of this traffic". Things were quite different when wheat was traded over long distances, because this always involved large quantities, and the risk was considerable. Only the really big merchants could raise the sums required, and only they could cope with the loss of a shipload if necessary. Under such circumstances, long-distance trade "engenders monopoly by its very nature". Accordingly, it became "an unrivalled machine for the rapid reproduction and increase of capital. In short, one is forced . . . [to see in] long-distance trade . . . an essential factor in the creation of merchant capitalism, and in the

creation of the merchant bourgeoisie" (Braudel 1983: 407f., 457). Put differently: as long-distance trade, even wheat became an urban affair. The extra
profits merchants could reap from the monopolies related to long-distance
trade poured into the city.

A lesson to be learnt from this example is that real (that is, big) profits
were only made where there was no (or very little) competition, i.e. *outside*
the market. Consequently, Braudel distinguishes two economic spheres, the
market economy where multiple actors were competing with each other,
and *capitalism*, which is characterized by monopolies and monopsonies
(Braudel 1983: 578). In line with the fact that medieval cities emerged as
socio-territorial monopolies, which promoted the activities and interests
of merchants and guilds, Braudel attributes to monopolies a central role in
explaining the economic strength of the towns. In addition to legal monopolies, granted by feudal authorities, came "actual" (Braudel 1983: 374) ones,
which seem to be even more important. Actual monopolies resulted from
cities' superior economic power, which in turn resulted from monopolistic
control of money (in large sums), monopolistic access to up-to-date and
diverse information, and monopolistic disposal over the skilled craftsmen.

Monopolistic control over money and, in particular, over money used as
credit plays a central role in Braudel's assessment of the production of uneven
development. To begin with, "money . . . was the active and decisive force"
(Braudel 1985: 511) behind the economic upswing, the urban renaissance
and the rural rearrangement from the eleventh century onwards. Since these
transformations heralded capitalist development, the ability to mobilize
money in sufficient quantities was pivotal for it. Braudel accordingly equates
capitalism with money economy, and, because money in larger quantities
was only found in cities, with "*urban* money": "Towns spelled money", and
vice versa: "money meant towns" (Braudel 1983: 249; 1984: 96; 1985: 511;
emphasis added; more on how this equation is arrived at below).

Because money was a preferred means to subjugate the country and its
producers, it became essential in the production of uneven development:
"There was not a town in Europe whose money did not spill out on to the
neighbouring land", and there are "plenty" of examples of how through this
spilling out of money "capitalism took over land and effectively subjected it
to its own rules" (Braudel 1983: 249, 251). Money was the means to create
access to the country, to penetrate the peasant societies, the "backward",
"pre-capitalist" economic spheres and to appropriate their products. And
this was crucial, because for Braudel capitalism thrives only by exploiting
inequalities (existing or those created over and over again). By "making use
both of the high voltage at the centre and of the weaknesses and compliance
of others", merchants' "success was only possible if the inferior and subject

economies were accessible, in various ways but on a regular basis, to the dominant economy" (Braudel 1984: 263).

In largely moneyless environs, "[t]he attraction in each case was ready cash" (Braudel 1985: 126). Having money meant enjoying an "actual" monopoly whose effect Braudel (1983: 59) compares to the explosive power of gunpowder: where money is rare, "it has a virtually explosive value". A traveller on such margins of the market economy, "with a few coins in his pocket, could procure all the riches of the earth at ridiculous prices". Money, thus, was used to set in motion the many and varied activities on a small scale of the peasant economy which were "trapped, imprisoned, unable to move from the ground". To mobilize it *from above*, all that was needed was "a little ready money, the silver coin that arrived at Danzig or Messina, the tempting offer of credit" (Braudel 1984: 44; emphasis in original). The pattern of domination exerted by dominant cities was the same everywhere: there were rural economies – Braudel actually calls them "market economy" – and there was urban capitalism "which seizes these humble activities from above, redirects them and holds them at its mercy. . . . The dominant economy thus embraced all production . . . . Any means that worked were used, in particular the granting of judicious credit" (*ibid.*: 38).

The often almost moneyless rural societies with their scarcity and risks depended on this credit, which, even worse, often came in the form of advance payments. Merchants "bought grain before it was harvested, wool before it was sheared, wine before the grapes were picked. And they controlled prices by hoarding foodstuffs; in the end they had the producer at their mercy" (Braudel 1983: 413; I shall return to discuss hoarding foodstuffs). The consequences for the peasants were in many cases disastrous because advance payments allowed merchants to bypass the market and its prices, for which reason "it was inevitable that one day 'vituperable' usury would be admitted in the open light of day" (Braudel 1983: 562).

Money, however, was weaponized not only against the immediate rural hinterland. It also served to subjugate overseas territories: "Money . . . is a means of exploiting someone else, at home or abroad" (Braudel 1985: 441). The actions of Portuguese merchants in Africa are described as follows: "Any and every means were indeed used to impose trading" including advance payments which had already proven their worth in Europe: if the debtor could not pay on time, the creditor had the right to seize the goods and eventually the person of the defaulter (Braudel 1984: 435). The same in Russia, where all the means Europe's merchants had at their disposal were "pressed into service", namely advance payments and the "European secret weapon, ready money" (*ibid.*: 462). Accordingly, it is the same process [that] can be observed everywhere: any society based on an ancient structure which opens its doors to money sooner or later loses its acquired equilibria and liberates forces that can never afterwards be adequately controlled. The new form of interchange disturbs the old order, benefits a few privileged individuals and hurts everyone else. . . . As a result, the extension of the monetary economy was a recurring drama quite as much in old countries accustomed to its presence as in those countries it reached without their immediately realizing it. (Braudel 1985: 437)

Monopolistic control of money, however, was not the only way through which cities shaped relations with the countryside unevenly and degraded it to their hinterland. The same was true for certain professions or skills. By attracting all the craftsmen the city created "for itself a monopoly of the manufacture and marketing of industrial products" (Braudel 1984: 94). Yet, in order to secure this monopoly, the attraction of skilled labour was accompanied by a ban on emigration and sometimes even bans on the sale of tools was just as necessary. In Nuremberg, for example, in the sixteenth and seventeenth centuries, ever more crafts were subject to such bans – spectacle makers, compass makers, brass burners and beaters, tinsmiths and hunting-horn makers (Reith 2014). The result, as already mentioned, was a division of labour in which the countryside was left only with the tasks that the city wanted to get rid of. On the other hand, towns monopolized professions that today we would classify as business services: the city "was of course the home of the men of law who wrote letters for the illiterate – and who were often false friends, masters of chicanery, or usurers who made the peasant sign IOUs, who charged high interest and seized goods left as security" (Braudel 1983: 258). In the French town of Varzy "[t]here were so many lawyers there that one wonders what they found to do – even when surrounded by an illiterate peasant population who obviously had to resort to the pens of others. But these lawyers were also landowners [and bourgeoisie, which is not directly evident from the quote, but the context in which it is placed]" (Braudel 1985: 482).

Why, however, was it that merchants were able to shape the division of labour in their own interests, exercise monopoly power and appropriate the fruits of other people's labour? What enabled certain European cities to gain and retain dominion over immediate and vast regions? While he specifies the urban environment(s) conducive to capitalism, Braudel does not reify cities. Even if his language sometimes seems to imply it, Braudel does not suggest that cities were actors, but their elites, which, however, are elite on the basis of their command over urban resources. With different weighting, agglomeration economies, external networks and the built environment always play a central role.

As to agglomerations, Braudel (1984: 31) highlights that cities were "high-tension system[s]" due to the quantity and diversity of people, money, knowledge, goods, services, etc., coming together in them. "Every town was a meeting-place for people and goods of all descriptions", he writes, and this was even more true for the real metropolises, which were "scene[s] of fantastic mixtures". Bigger cities even represented "unusual concentration[s]", with the resulting social diversification becoming a source of wealth, vitality and innovative power (Braudel 1985: 503; 1984: 30; 1985: 481).

Perhaps the most important "thing" that was unusually concentrated in cities – and particularly in the big, important ones – was money. We have already seen that Braudel equates capitalism with "urban money", and there are good reasons for this. As banal as it may sound, a key agglomeration exter-nality that medieval cities produced was that they helped to make money *available*. This should certainly be understood in the very physical sense, i.e. as the availability of moneybags full of coins. In times when paper money, deposit banking and payment and credit systems over distance were only beginning (not to mention financial markets and digital money, of course), access to the physical means of payment was key. "[R]eady money", writes Braudel (1984: 462), was the "secret weapon" with which advance payments could be made, which in turn were, as we have seen, the means to seize the humble activities of the peasant economy. The physical existence of "ready money" had, of course, a geographical implication: money was where those who possessed it lived. In the late Middle Ages and early modern period, these were the merchants, particularly those engaged in long-distance trade, and industrialists. Both congregated in cities. The urbanization of key economic actors and of money went hand in hand, and this is why Braudel (1983: 416) equates having "sufficient capital" with having access to "local sources of credit". Given that having "enough credit . . . is power" (Braudel 1984: 245), co-location with actors with money at their disposal translates into a strategic advantage, into a weapon. Cities' "monetary *stock*" is one of the "instruments of capitalism" because it "combined mass and momentum. If the mass increased or the overall momentum was accelerated, the result was virtually the same: everything went up: prices, more slowly wages, and the total volume of transactions" (Braudel 1985: 476; emphasis added). The more money one could mobilize, the better, because the "really big profits were only attainable by capitalists who handled large sums of money – their own or other people's" (Braudel 1983: 432).

Yet, the easy availability of credit stimulated business and encouraged the rhythm of accumulation not only by allowing for an increase in the volume of transactions. Being able to draw on "monetary stock[s]" was also an essential part of capitalist success because it enabled merchants to choose between opportunities, and having a choice allowed them "to break into a resistant circuit, to defend a threatened advantage, to make good one's losses, to ward off rivals; it meant being in a position to wait for returns which were slow, but promising . . . Last but not least, it meant the freedom to obtain even more" (Braudel 1983: 384). In the light of Braudel's understanding of capitalism, which sees capital's greatest secret of success in its "unlimited flexibility, its capacity for change and adaptation . . . its capacity to slip at a moment's notice from one form or sector to another, in times of crisis or of pronounced decline in profit rates" (*ibid.*: 433), the freedom of action that access to money implied guaranteed a big competitive advantage. One, however, only few enjoyed, amongst them, for example, Amsterdam-based merchants. Braudel quotes Accarias de Serionne, an eighteenth-century scholar: "If ten or twelve Businessmen of Amsterdam of the first rank meet for a banking [i.e. a credit] operation, they can in a moment send circulating throughout Europe over two hundred million florins . . . There is no Sovereign who could do as much . . . This credit is a power which the ten or twelve businessmen will be able to exert over all the states in Europe, in complete independence of any authority" (1984: 245).

Providing access to money was, however, not the only advantage that the agglomeration offered to early capitalist actors. Part of cities' being "high-tension system[s]" was that they are information-rich environments – information about markets were available faster there, in greater quantity and variability, and hence more reliably. On the one hand, this was due to the fact that many people from different regions with different views of the world met in cities, which increased the amount of information available and sharpened its interpretation. On the other hand, big cities attracted information, simply because they were better connected, with "better" meaning "more" (having roads, for example, to more different places) as well as "faster". As to the latter, Braudel notes that "[i]f big cities attracted rapid news in their direction it was because they paid for speed and always had the means to create better communications, one of which was obviously to build stone or paved roads" (1985: 424). Investing in the built environment was thus a means of gaining a lead in access to information.

Due to the greater amount and superior trustworthiness of information, capitalist actors in major cities enjoyed a competitive advantage. They learned in time and received accurate information about harvests, prices, famines, and they profited from this knowledge by switching to the economic sectors and regions where profits were highest. Therefore, for merchants it was the prime requirement to be included in "as many as possible of the information networks which advised one where there was a promising opportunity, or on the contrary which should be avoided like the plague". Having a "strategic position" in a good communications network was an "inestimable advantage", all the more "at a time when news travelled very slowly and at great cost". And of course, here too, monopoly played an important role: "[t]he most advantageous information was something that no one else knew". If one takes the two agglomeration externalities mentioned here, which were produced by the late medieval and early modern city together, the conclusion is obvious: only those capitalist actors who were "both sufficiently informed and materially able to choose the sphere of its action" (who had, in other words, accurate news and monetary stocks at their disposal) could become successful (Braudel 1983: 410, 400).

The latter example shows that when we speak of agglomeration and its externalities we must also speak of inter-city networks. Everything Braudel writes about the amassing of money in cities or about their informational advantage proves that cities "are essentially open; they are meeting places . . . [t]hey pull into themselves" (Massey *et al.* 1999: 2). Cities are agglomerations because they are nodes in regional and supra-regional networks – without merchants' extensive networks, connecting them to other metropolises, smaller towns and villages, none of the agglomeration externalities mentioned could have been achieved: "Every town was a meeting-place for people and goods of all descriptions: each product linked it to a given area of the surrounding neighbourhood and sometimes to places far away. Each instance demonstrates how urban life was connected with such areas which only partly overlapped" (Braudel 1985: 503).

Cities, according to Braudel, do not come into being of their own accord, and even less they can survive of their own accord. Cities exist only as components of networks that include a central, dominant city, and second- and third-tier ones, down to small villages and hamlets. From everywhere economic life is breathed into the city: food, labour, money, raw materials for craft and industry, trade goods. Whereas inter-city networks are a necessity for the survival of every town, the capitalist city Braudel deals with needed them particularly because long-distance trade was its most profitable business. For long-distance trade, however, control of extended trade routes was a prerequisite, and this could only be achieved through wide-ranging inter-city networks. Braudel rhetorically asks whether long-distance connections could be linked and controlled by "huge headquarters" at home, or "were there . . . subsidiary centres?". Of course the latter, because merchants needed "to have associates at strategic points along the trade route, who were a party to one's secrets", they "could not do without a network of reliable go-betweens and associates" (Braudel 1983: 157, 416, 150). Accordingly, "[t]here could be no world economy until there was a dense enough urban network with trade of sufficient volume and regularity to breathe life into a central or core zone" (Braudel 1984: 96). An early example of this is the Hanseatic League's network of cities and trade that integrated Western, Northern and Eastern Europe; a later one that reached from Amsterdam westward via Madrid, Seville and Cadiz to the American colonies, and in today's Mexico via Veracruz, Mexico City, Zacatecas to the silver mining regions in central Mexico, and eastward via Gdansk to towns and villages to present-day Poland. Yet, not only grain, fish, timber and plundered silver circulated in and through these networks, but also knowledge. Innovations in finance (a sector to which Braudel attributes great importance) are a case in point. They "spread from city to city", with the merchants themselves being the bearers of the information and thereby drivers of innovation. Traveling from city to city, merchants could automatically, unintentionally observe what others do or know. Taking the case of the bill of exchange as an example, they *could not* "have failed to notice this convenient method of transferring a sum of money to distant parts simply by a piece of paper" (Braudel 1983: 556).

In sum, "[n]ews, merchandise, capital, credit, people, instructions, correspondence all flow into and out of the city" (Braudel 1984: 27). Yet, what is crucial for the topic of this book is that these inter-city networks have been crucial for the functioning of the capitalist world economy in all respects. Not only did they enable trade and the economic prosperity it drove, but also the exploitation that was, according to Braudel, inextricably linked to it. Inter-city networks were therefore, contrary to what the word "networks" would suggest, always hierarchic, serving the purpose of centripetal wealth transfers. Accordingly, the towns around the centre had to play "the role of associate or accomplice, but more usually [they are] resigned to their second-class role. Their activities are governed by those of the metropolis: they stand guard around it, direct the flow of business toward it, redistribute or pass on the goods it sends them, live off its credit or suffer its rule (Braudel 1984: 27). For Braudel, this hierarchization of space belongs to his "ground rules" of capitalism.

The inequality of relationships characterizes even the most elementary networks. I have already quoted Braudel on the notion that any "town only exists as a town in relation to a form of life lower than its own". To this he adds:

There are no exceptions to this rule. . . . There is no town, no townlet without its villages, its scrap of rural life attached. . . . So

urban history has to be extended to cover these small communities, for little towns, as Spengler observed, eventually 'conquer'
the surrounding countryside ... meanwhile being themselves
devoured and subordinated by agglomerations more populous
and more active. Such towns are thus caught up into urban systems orbiting regularly round some sun-city. But it would be a
mistake only to count the sun-cities – Venice, Florence, Nuremberg, Lyons, Amsterdam, London, Delhi, Nanking, Osaka. *Towns
form hierarchies everywhere*, but the tip of the pyramid does not
tell us everything, important though it may be. (Braudel 1985:
481–3; emphasis added)

The ultimate rationale of inter-city networks was to provide a socio-
physical infrastructure stretched over space to make the submission and
exploitation of other regions possible. The urban network Europe developed
was "*an urban superstructure*, with inter-city links encompassing all underlying activities and obliging them to become part of a 'market economy'"
(Braudel 1984: 96; emphasis added). Note that "market economy" is within
quotation marks – a reference to the still modest scale of transactions,
but also to the fact that these in many cases were shaped not according to
the market, but by urban monopolists. In this way, "[t]he spreading [city]
network conquered one territory after another and created a hierarchy of
regions" (*ibid.*: 322). Inter-city networks were "like a vast net thrown over
the wealth of the other continents" (Braudel 1985: 457). Without "satellites
and the nervous system of urban relay points" (*ibid.*: 150) surplus could not
be syphoned off from other regions and transferred to the centres, but with
it, "[t]he western town swallowed everything, forced everything to submit
to its laws, its demands and its controls". In this way, the "*Fernhändler* was
... appropriating the surplus-value of the worker in the mines or plantations,
or that of the primitive peasant on the Malabar Coast or the East Indies"
(Braudel 1983: 27, 404f.; emphasis in original. *Fernhändler* means distant
merchant). In sum, of the trading networks established from the fifteenth
century onwards, "cities were at once the instruments, the articulations and
the beneficiaries" (Braudel 1984: 92).

Europe's overseas expansions and (economic) conquests are a good
example of how inter-city networks functioned. From the European perspective, Seville and Cadiz were "the bridgeheads to America", so that a "command
structure [that] ran from Madrid to Seville and thence to the New World"
was established. As to the colonial plantation economies in the Americas,
"[e]verything was remote-controlled", from Seville and Cadiz, Bordeaux,
Nantes and Rouen, Amsterdam, Bristol and Liverpool (Braudel 1983: 152,

176, 272). On the other side of the Atlantic, however, there were also bridge-heads. In the colonies, the people forced to work were ruled and exploited by "the mother country, determined to preserve for itself all the trading profits deriving from the monopoly it always exercised". Yet, because this mother country had been far away, "cities and local elites controlled affairs on the spot". Although subordinated to actors and cities in the mother countries, the bridgeheads or "'entry points' are quite evidently part and parcel of capitalism", too, because without them, effective exploitation would not have been feasible (Braudel 1984: 53, 65).

What arises from such a perspective is a *citified* concept of how the unevenness of capitalism was produced. Braudel (1984: 48) denotes its division of labour "as a chain of subordinations, each conditioning the others". And he stresses the structural inequality of and dependence within this division of labour, for example, when he refers to Amsterdam's grain trade with Eastern Europe. Explaining an illustration, he notes that the Polish and Western merchants were "the men who forged the chain of dependence linking Poland to Amsterdam" (Braudel 1984: 48f.). The more important, dynamic and central a city, the more subordinates it had. The real metropolis – cities like Venice, Antwerp or Amsterdam – "came accompanied by a train of subordinates" – indeed, "its retinue of assistants and subordinates" was "the first sign by which it could be recognized" (Braudel 1984: 30). This gives Braudel a methodological clue for the analysis of capitalism. We have to see, he asserts,

> how this entire network, which I see as a superstructure, connected at lower levels with lesser economies. It is with these connections, meeting-points and multiple links that we shall be particularly concerned, since they reveal the way in which a dominant economy can exploit subordinate economies, while not soiling its own hands with the less profitable activities or types of production, or even, most of the time, directly supervising the lesser links in the chain of trade. (*ibid.*: 248)

Ultimately, Braudel emphasizes the massiveness of the built environment in cities as an essential means to merchants' capability to drive accumulation and uneven development. When Braudel (1984: 36) writes about "the construction process of any world economy", this must not be understood figuratively. Every economy requires physical infrastructure, and so Braudel's references to the built environment are innumerable: to marketplaces (increasingly covered with the growth of trade), exchanges, shops, butcheries, barracks; to streets, avenues and fleets; to ports, docks, pools, basins and quays; and of course to the *kontors*,[22] stores, depots, granaries and warehouses of Europe's merchants. A leading city such as Venice additionally counted on a mint (the Zecca), the palace of the political authority (Palazzo Ducale, the Doge's residence and the seat of Venetian government), and industrial facilities, mainly for war purposes (the Arsenale di Venezia, made of shipyards and armaments factories). *Physical* construction processes therefore underly the building up of a world economy.

Given Braudel's focus on trade, it is no wonder that he draws particular attention to its material infrastructure. Warehouses play a particular role. Behind the Hanseatic League, he contends, there was no state, not even a firmly-constituted organization, but just towns. These, however, could count on their "merchants, its patricians, its guilds, fleet, warehouses and accumulated wealth" (Braudel 1984: 103). As for Amsterdam, he asserts that its means to gain superiority was a great mass of money in constant circulation (an aspect we have already dealt with), and having all goods available at any time. The latter, however, required storage facilities. And Amsterdam was set up to be able to fulfil this condition. In the early eighteenth century, Braudel (1983: 96) quotes a contemporary source, a large number of vessels arrived every day, and so it is easy to understand "why there are a great number of warehouses and cellars to hold all the merchandise carried by these ships: so the city is well provided with them, having whole districts which consist of warehouses or granaries, from five to eight storeys high, and besides that, most houses along the canals have two or three store-rooms and a cellar". And Braudel continues:

> [T]he warehouses of Amsterdam could absorb and then disgorge any amount of goods. . . . the crucial elements in Amsterdam's role [were] collecting, storing, selling and re-selling the goods of the universe. It was a policy which had already been practised by Venice; . . . This storage capacity undoubtedly seemed by the standards of the time excessive and indeed pernicious, since the force of attraction could lead to quite ridiculous itineraries for the merchandise. . . . Storage and warehousing lay at the heart of Dutch commercial strategy. (1984: 236–8)

---

22. *Kontors* were Hanseatic trading-posts in London, Bruges, Bergen and Novgorod. They were a legal institution endowed with certain trading privileges, but inextricably linked to specific buildings: in Novgorod the Peterhof, in Bergen the Tyske Bryggen, in London the Stalhof and in Bruges the Hansekontor.

Thanks to this infrastructure, all kinds of products from all over the world could be temporarily stored in Amsterdam before being resold at a profit: tobacco, sugar, grain, pewter, cloth, coffee, and much more. So, just as we have said that agglomeration can only be created through networks, networks can only exist through the built environment. While it is true that "maritime traffic made Amsterdam 'the warehouse of the World'", as Braudel (1984: 184) quotes another contemporary source, it is also true that maritime traffic could enrich Amsterdam only because the city's author-ities and private merchants have had sufficient storage space built. Braudel even contends that in the seventeenth century, the "great warehouses" of the Oost Indische Companie formed the "*real* centre" of the global pepper trade (1983: 193; emphasis added). Amsterdam, in a word, practised "'ware-house trade'" (*ibid.*: 141). And of course, agglomeration economies needed the built environment, too. When Braudel (1984: 236) affirms that in "Amsterdam, everything was crammed together, concentrated: the ships in the harbour, . . . the merchants who thronged to the Bourse, and the goods which piled up in warehouses only to pour out of them", then a port with docks and wharves was needed, a building for the stock exchanges, and the warehouses that Braudel himself mentions.

Of course, warehouses were not a privilege of Amsterdam. Whether in port cities such as Cadiz, Lisbon, Liverpool or Marseilles, or in cities along rivers – London, of course, but also smaller ones such as Lille, Mulhouse or Mainz – everywhere was "[t]he Europe of fairs . . . turning into the Europe of warehouses" (Braudel 1983: 96). While the growing trade demanded a corresponding infrastructure, warehouses in some cases served a purpose beyond simple storage. For Braudel, real capitalism begins beyond the market economy and is determined by monopolistic practices – he speaks of "any world economy, with its inbuilt monopolies" (Braudel 1984: 36). These depended on political power, but not only. Rather, physical infrastruc-tures played a crucial role, too, and this is where the warehouses come in. Merchants who sought to pursue monopolies needed not only large sums of money (their own or borrowed) and extensive inter-city networks, but also storage facilities. One of the secrets of the Hanseatic merchants' success was "to control both supply and demand whether for exports to the West or redis-tribution of imports within the East". For such policies, the Hanseatic *kontors* "were strongholds . . . protected by privilege and defended to the utmost" (Braudel 1984: 103). For the seventeenth-century's Dutch merchants, who were "masters of the art" of creating monopolies, the

[p]ractical weapons for such monopolies were the great ware-houses . . . which could hold enough grain to feed the United

Provinces for ten or twelve years as well as herrings and spices, English cloth and French wines, saltpetre from Poland or the East Indies, Swedish copper, tobacco from Maryland, cocoa from Venezuela, Russian furs and Spanish wool, hemp from the Baltic and silk from the Levant. The rule was always the same: buy goods directly from the producer for a low price, in return for cash or, better still, advance payments; then put them in store and wait for prices to rise (or give them a push). (Braudel 1983: 418f.)

For those who could store goods – particularly grain – and therefore were in no hurry to resell, there were many opportunities to speculate on price increases. War, for example, "always meant that foreign goods became scarce and went up in price", for which reason the merchants "crammed their five- or six-storey warehouses to bursting-point". Famines were good times for merchants, too. In such times, wheat became "a 'royal' merchandise", with profit rates jumping up to 300 per cent (while normally for bulk goods 5 per cent was good). The warehouse was thus inevitable in order to turn goods with use values into pure speculative objects that served capitalism's endless accumulation of capital: "[H]oarded in a warehouse . . . this cereal changed its nature: it was now a counter in a complicated game which only rich merchants could play" (Braudel 1983: 419, 405, 455). Not only are hoarding and usury siblings, the warehouse is also part of the family: "[I]f Amsterdam called the tune for European prices . . . it was because of the abundance of reserve stocks which the city's warehouses could at any moment release or hold back" (Braudel 1984: 239). And of course, the monopoly–warehouse combination also served colonialism. French activities in the Caribbean, for example, were based on the fact that the colonizers "obliged the islanders to use the services of their boats, their captains [. . .] their warehouses and their life-saving advance payments. [These] were thus the masters of the machine that turned out the riches of the colonies" (ibid.: 277).

The function cities had in organizing colonial exploitation, and how this continued to shape the role of cities in the former colonies even after political independence, has been discussed in the literatures on urbanization in Latin America and Asia. I shall examine important contributions from this work in the next section.

CITIES AS "SUCTION PUMPS":[23] THE POLITICAL
ECONOMY OF PERIPHERAL URBANIZATION

The city has not always had the good reputation it has today. From the mid-1950s and continuing through the 1970s, scholars from fields as diverse as development economics, urban planning and radical political economy, began to question the prevailing modernization-theoretical consensus that urbanization and economic development were interdependent processes. These critical scholars included both people with a theoretical background in the prevailing modernization theories of the time as well as Marxists and other intellectual currents critical of capitalism. The trigger for these doubts was that it became increasingly obvious that the modernization-theoretical promise that all countries could become "like the West" would not be fulfilled. High rates of population growth coupled with rapid urbanization in the de-colonized or decolonizing world, an often primate city distribution, the lack of industrial employment in the cities, a pronounced polarization between urban and rural areas, and widespread urban informality in the big cities raised, as Castells (1977: 39) put it, "practical, that is to say political" concerns about the relationship between development and urbanization. A debate on urban overpopulation became heated; that the cities of the then still called "Third World" were "over-urbanized" became a common credo which was based mainly on the observed mismatch between urban population and industrial jobs. The inability of the then mainstream urban theories to explain the differences between urbanization in Latin America and Asia and that in the USA or Western Europe led to discontent amongst (younger) scholars and to a drive for a renewal in urban studies. What caused a great deal of debate was the question of why, although cities in the peripheries grew rapidly, there was no wide-ranging generative growth effect of cities on the economy of their countries. The genius of cities had seemingly stopped working.

Parallel to this unrest in urban studies, and indeed also linked to it, a paradigm shift in the wider social sciences occurred. Scholars drew attention to the fact that uneven development (at various scales, from regional to global) seemed to persist, and that is why it became theorized as a dynamic inherent to capitalism. Accordingly, both the development optimism of modernization theory and the equilibrium assumption of neoclassical economics were discarded. Dependency theory and world-systems analysis brought a further far-reaching innovation, namely the rejection of methodological nationalism.

---

23. Timberlake (1987: 51).

Contending that capitalism is a global, all-pervasive system, they argued that there could be no independent "national" or "regional" (and, for that matter, "urban") developments. Accordingly, social scientists were required to keep the "whole" in mind, even when analysing individual phenomena or processes such as urbanization.

As a result of these developments, new paradigms emerged in urban studies, namely "new urban sociology" and "urban political economy" (for seminal contributions, see Harvey 1973, Portes & Walton 1976, Castells 1977 and Roberts 1978). These two paradigms agree on essential conceptual points: first, urbanization, cities and the networks they form have to be interpreted as part of wider societal structures and processes, namely capitalism. Therefore, both approaches put cities in a historical as well as in a global perspective (rather than a presentist and national one), focusing on transformations over time and their relations to a city's position in the global division of labour. This implies that urban processes and phenomena will differ in different regions, according to their specific position in the world-system – a contention in direct contradiction to modernization theory. Second, both the new urban sociology and urban political economy drew attention to the interests of different social groups in the context of urbanization and, related to this, to inequality and conflicts. Yet, the two approaches also differ in some respects: whereas the former is strongly influenced by classical Marxist political economy, the latter draws heavily on dependency theory and particularly on world-systems analysis. This difference becomes visible above all in the chosen geographical focus: new urban sociology is mainly concerned with cities in the centres of the world economy (mostly in the USA), whereas urban political economy is concerned with urbanization processes and cities in the peripheries (and here mainly in Latin America). Typical topics also differ to some extent. Although both currents are concerned with poverty and housing problems, new urban sociology focuses more on segregation, deindustrialization, austerity programmes and fiscal crises, and urban political economy on the lack of (industrial) employment, informality and inadequate infrastructure in "Third World" cities.

Due to their geographical focus on cities in the peripheries, scholars from the ranks of urban political economy were concerned not with the role of cities in development, but in just the opposite, in the "development of underdevelopment" (Frank 1969). This city-critical perspective derived from conceptual notions of dependency theory and world-systems analysis, namely: (1) poverty and socio-spatial polarization are the results of uneven development, i.e. of historical processes in which exploitative relationships at national, regional and global levels have produced centres and peripheries; and (2) the adequate unit of analysis for all social phenomena, processes and relations is capitalism as a worldwide system and not individual countries or regions. Accordingly, cities can only be understood in the light of their integration into the global division of labour. There is yet a third influence of dependency theory and world-systems analysis, and this is critical to my argument because it suggests cities' proactivity in the production of uneven development. Both theories reject the endogenous–exogenous dualism established in the social sciences as a product of methodological nationalism. This dualism constructs a worldview in which "inside" (within the nation state that is being examined) and "outside" (the rest of the world) are clearly separated from each other; recognizable in the distinction between the "domestic market" and the "world economy", or between "national politics" and "international relations". This is misleading, even wrong, because, as dependency-theorist Osvaldo Sunkel put it: "[F]oreign factors are seen not as external but as intrinsic to the system . . . [in] the underdeveloped country. These contribute significantly to shaping the nature and operation of the economy, society and polity" (1972: 519). Accordingly, the "inside" is shaped by the "outside", while the "outside" is produced and reproduced by the "inside". In the study of cities, it follows that just as there are no domestic markets or national policies, there are neither national urban systems nor national hierarchies of cities. If we have established with Brian Berry (1964: 160f.) that "[t]he most immediate part of the environment of any city is other cities", then this is not limited to cities "in their own country". Exactly as in the capitalist division of labour, where the relations between enterprises and between enterprises and workers are (potentially) global, so too are the relations that form and hold together inter-city networks global (as we have already seen in detail in Braudel's work). From this, two far-reaching conclusions can be drawn for our topic.

First, exploitation across space – be it at the national, regional or global scale – does not work simply through spatial contrasts, as formulations such as North versus South, or USA versus Mexico might suggest. If the internal–external dualism does not exist, then neither do the North and the South exist as separate, independent entities. Accordingly, exploitation, even when organized across space, is always internal, namely within the global capitalist division of labour. Differentiations, which are commonly addressed with "North" and "South" or "core" (or "centre") and "periphery", do exist, of course, but within the worldwide division of labour. They are connected through commodity chains, which serve not only as infrastructure of production and trade, but also as pipelines through which wealth transfers from the peripheries to the cores are accomplished. However, in order for centripetal wealth transfers to work, intermediaries along the way are needed. These intermediaries are social actors (as merchants in Gdansk, who assisted Amsterdam's merchants in Braudel's examples, or, more recently, "foreign" branches of transnational corporations and "national" companies in a country like Mexico). However, the notion of intermediaries also refers to geographical entities, and that is where cities come into play. As we know from Braudel (1984: 30; 1985: 150), a metropolis, in order to be a metropolis at all, needs "train[s] of subordinates", and uneven development functions through "satellites and the nervous system of urban relay points". Exploitation across space does actually not work *across* space but *through* it, namely through networks of cities that span across national boundaries.

The second conclusion to be drawn from the non-existence of an inside–outside dualism and the fact that the "foreign" is intrinsic to the "domestic" – to paraphrase Sunkel (1972) – is that many elements of the overall system have an ambiguous character. In particular the intermediaries act in two directions, inwards and outwards, or, if we refer to uneven development, "up and down". Cities, accordingly, are both exploited themselves (by the more powerful), and actively involved in the exploitation of other cities and of their hinterland. Cities therefore operate as hinges, they are bridgeheads of higher-level economic actors and their entry gates into the areas to be exploited. André Gunder Frank has vividly described this structure with reference to Latin America, and it is worth quoting him at length:

[T]hese metropolis-satellite relations are not limited to the imperial or international level but penetrate and structure the very economic, political, and social life of the Latin American colonies and countries. Just as the colonial and national capital ... become the satellite of the Iberian (and later of other) metropoles of the world economic system, this satellite immediately becomes a colonial and then a national metropolis with respect to the productive sectors and population of the interior. Furthermore, the provincial capitals, which thus are themselves satellites of the national metropolis – and through the latter of the world metropolis – are in turn provincial centers around which their own local satellites orbit. Thus, *a whole chain of constellations of metropoles and satellites relates all parts of the whole system* from its metropolitan center in Europe or the United States to the farthest outpost in the Latin American countryside. When we examine this metropolis-satellite structure, we find that *each of the satellites ... serves as an instrument to suck capital or economic surplus out of its own satellites and to channel part of this surplus to the world metropolis of which all are satellites.* Moreover, each national and local metropolis serves to impose and maintain the monopolistic structure and exploitative relationship of this system . . . as long as it serves the interests of the metropoles which take advantage of this global, national, and local structure to promote their own development and the enrichment of their ruling classes. (1969: 6f.; all emphases added)

However lucid Frank's description is, the debate on the exploitative role of cities in peripheral countries – in colonial times, but, very importantly, also after political independence – was not started by dependency theorists. The first to make this position widely heard was Bert Hoselitz, economist and social scientist at the University of Chicago (and, coincidently or not, supervisor of Frank's PhD thesis).[24] Hoselitz, who himself had an intellectual affinity for modernization theory, had already questioned in the 1950s the equation of urbanization and economic development with his highly regarded essay, "Generative and Parasitic Cities" (Hoselitz 1955).

For Hoselitz, the decisive point was not that a city extracted surplus from surrounding regions; as a modernization theorist, he took that as a prerequisite for economic development. His concern instead focused on how cities used this soaked-up surplus. Whereas Hoselitz assumed that cities usually multiply it, contributing thereby to national growth – hence, the designation as a "generative city" – he also acknowledged that there can be cases when such an evolutionist perspective on urbanization does not apply. During colonialism, economic development remained limited to a central city without stimulating growth in the entire region, which is why the major city is considered "parasitic". It siphons off the surplus nationwide which then is consumed within the city or forwarded elsewhere, without providing "development" at the origin of the surplus. The same can happen in independent, but underdeveloped countries, just as when a city acquires a strong position of primacy. Whereas Hoselitz (1955: 294; emphasis added) adopts the terminology of time ("a series of at least temporary parasitic influences [are] exerted by the *primate city*"), he attributes this parasitism to a factor that has nothing to do with primacy at all, but is very close to what his student Frank was to formulate a decade later. Cities in underdeveloped countries, Hoselitz suggests, become parasitic because they function as bridgeheads for foreign interests. As the dominant powers' "gateways to the hinterland which they dominate", main cities have enabled the "excessive depletion of natural resources, and the exploitation of peasants and other primary producers".

---

24. I thank Michiel van Meeteren for pointing this out to me.

Therefore, while they are themselves "subordinate to the great centres of world trade", colonial cities reproduced global unevenness on a regional scale, functioning as hinges between the local, regional and global scales of colonial exploitation (Hoselitz 1955: 284, 280). Accordingly, "internal" and "external" unevenness overlapped and reinforced each other – uneven regional development was the result not only of "external" dependence of and exploitation by the colonial power, but was also "internally" co-produced in the main city or cities.

Another voice to draw attention early on to the negative role of (capital) cities in processes of uneven development is that of urban planner John Friedmann, founder of the Program for Urban Planning in the Graduate School of Architecture and Planning at UCLA and, at least in the early part of his career, like Hoselitz neither an ally of dependency theory nor of world-systems analysis. Originally sharing modernization theory's notion that the diffusion of innovation and economic growth works through a country's urban hierarchy, trickling down from the top, from the largest metropolis to the smaller cities, towns and the countryside, Friedmann's professional experience in non-core countries led him to break from this belief. He contended that a country's core region(s), and by this he meant the capital and other major cities, may be unwilling to use surpluses that have been appropriated from the whole country to develop this. Rather, the main cities "*impose* a condition of *organized* dependency on their peripheries ... [they] *organize* the periphery as a continuing source of supply of raw materials, food stuffs, and semi-processed goods, ... [and they] *organize* the periphery as a set of market areas" (Friedmann 1967: 23, 30; emphases added). Friedmann thus considered regional socio-spatial polarization in peripheral countries not as a temporary byproduct of development, but rather as an active process, as the generation of uneven development prompted by a country's core region(s). The major city conditions the development of the peripheral areas in such a way that their structure becomes oriented towards the needs of the centre, which naturally hampers regional development. For Friedmann, developing countries therefore typically create a spatial system that reflects "a dominant and *persisting pattern of nonreciprocal exchange relations among cities and regions*" (Friedmann 1973: 38; emphasis added).

A further contribution, critical of the equation of urbanization and economic development, but outside the intellectual spheres of dependency theory and world-systems analysis-influenced researchers, is Michael Lipton's (1977) "urban bias" thesis. He argues that poverty in poor countries persists because their governments favour cities through biased resource allocation and price policies. Accordingly, for Lipton, the "most important class conflict in the poor countries . . . is not between labour and capital. Nor is it between foreign and national interests. It is between the *rural classes* and the *urban classes*" (*ibid.*: 13; emphasis added).

Urban political economy's critical stance towards cities' role in the development (or underdevelopment) stemmed from thorough examination with the colonization of Latin America. True to their convictions that cities – and urbanization in general – can only be understood as part of their function in the global division of labour, and that political and economic interests of actors and groups of actors play an important role in how cities and inter-city networks develop, scholars aligned to this approach focused their interest on two topics: the role of the cities founded by the Spanish and Portuguese colonizers or "taken over" from the Aztecs (e.g. Tenochtitlan, today's Mexico City) or Incas (e.g. Cusco, in present-day Peru) in strategies of colonial conquest and exploitation; and how this specific role shaped the "internal" development of cities in terms of their economic activity, social structure, spatial organization and built environment.

As far as the first aspect is concerned, there is a broad consensus that "[u]rban development was an integral part of both Spanish and Portuguese colonization" and that the system of cities that the colonizers developed had as its "main object to control and administrate the new domains" (Roberts 1978: 37). In the same vein, Portes (1977: 60–64; emphasis added) speaks of an "urban-centered strategy of colonization", that cities "were means for conquest and control of the wealth of the new countries", and even that "[c]ities offered the *only* setting where an exploitative orientation could be implemented successfully". From the defeated and occupied "capital" cities of the old empires, conquest and subjugation moved inland and towards the coasts. "On the way" existing settlements were taken over and new cities founded. With regard to the latter, two motives prevailed: on the one hand, military bases were created. Because the territories to be conquered were unknown and inhabited by populations hostile to the Spanish and Portuguese, and because personnel imposing European authority was relatively small compared to the size of the territory, it had to be concentrated in a few strategic places. On the other hand, cities were founded for economic – or, as Portes (*ibid.*) says repeatedly, "predatory" – reasons. This was the case in the mining regions (e.g. Potosí in today's Bolivia); where fertile land and the presence of indigenous populations, whose labour could be exploited, made agriculture a feasible venture (e.g. Santa María la Antigua del Darién in present-day Colombia); and, of course, where the coast's natural bays suggested the creation of harbours, which were necessary for shipping minerals (silver) or agricultural goods (sugar) to Europe (e.g. La Habana, Cuba). Gradually, the cities expanded their operational capacity to become political, economic, religious and cultural sub-centres that enabled the permanent integration of large swathes of land and the people living there. To be sure, "integration" meant nothing other than control, making the indigenous population available for exploitation and indoctrination. Neither the Spanish Crown nor the conquistadors (mostly minor nobles and military officers) could have achieved this exclusively from Mexico City or Lima (the capital of the Viceroyalty of Peru), let alone from Madrid. Accordingly, social intermediaries were required (a role that was to be assumed by the Ladino or Mestizo people) along with geographical intermediaries – cities – which acted as gateways into hinterlands, as door-openers or more aptly, as burglars. What Portes (*ibid.*: 63) calls "the urban strategy of colonization" corresponds to Braudel's (1985: 150) metropolis' need of a "nervous system of urban relay points" for the purpose of exploiting "foreign" territories, and to what Frank (1969: 6) had called the "whole chain of constellations of metropoles and satellites . . . [which] . . . relates all parts of the whole system from its metropolitan centre in Europe or the United States to the farthest outpost in the Latin American countryside".

Cities in colonial Latin America arose neither as market places, as a necessity born out of increasing trade, nor as production sites. Cities in fertile regions, for example, did not grow progressively, in tandem with increased agricultural production and trade. Not even did colonial cities emerge and grow, as can be argued for the European cities, due to uneven relationships with the hinterland. Rather, they were founded by the "exterland" (Pasquel 1958; quoted in Morse 1971: 5), with the purpose to subsequently establish these uneven relations. Their *raison d'être* was to organize and to control the exploitation of mines and agriculture, and ultimately the exploitation of the Indigenous people. Brazilian sugar plantations, for example, though at first glance isolated and self-sufficient, were remote- (that is city-) controlled, and the profits they generated were "distributed by means of these urban centres to government, merchants and the church" (Roberts 1978: 42). Cities owned their hinterlands both in formal-legal terms (land was granted in the Crown's name by city authorities to settlers) and in de facto terms of economic and political control. Colonial cities, in a word, "did not arise to serve, but to subdue" (Portes 1977: 60). From the very beginning, their existence and the character they possessed were part of a deeply uneven, asymmetrical relationship to rural areas which established "the supremacy of city over countryside . . . conquerors lived, by and large, in the city, while conquered remained in the countryside" (*ibid.*).

So, colonial cities were instruments of wealth creation, but in a very different sense than we understand it today, thinking of cities as highly productive, efficient and innovative environments. Colonial cities' mission was to organize wealth production *outside* themselves, in mines and fields, produced by and appropriated from those who did not live in the city but in villages and hamlets (the Indigenous people). Unlike the late medieval cities in (Western) Europe, the colonial city in Latin America "was the energy and organization for the exploitation of natural resources", as Morse (1962: 474) noted. Yet, the city not only served for the exploitation of natural resources, but also for the organization of centripetal wealth flows resulting from this exploitation. Although some of the wealth that flowed out of the indigenous villages and hamlets was appropriated by provincial towns, more remained in the colonial capital and most ended up in a European metropolis (in reality much of the silver that arrived in Madrid did *not* end up there but was almost immediately drained to Amsterdam –this is another story [Arrighi 1994]). While in sixteenth- and seventeenth-century Europe the growing wealth of the incipient nations came not from the nations themselves, but from cities, in Latin America the wealth came from rural areas and populations and was syphoned off and channelled by local cities to the European cities. The dynamics of the latter was therefore by no means only attributable to their own genius.

The role of colonial cities as links in chains of exploitation and centripetal wealth transfers, however, shaped their internal social structure and their own economic dynamics. Firstly, the colonial towns were insignificant in terms of population. As late as 1950, only a quarter of Latin America's population lived in cities with more than 20,000 inhabitants, and for cities with more than 100,000, the share was only 17 per cent (Hauser 1961: 96). More important than the demographic insignificance, however, was that the cities remained economically unimportant, at least as long as we understand the "economic significance of the city" in the sense that it is widely used today, as an engine of growth (that cities, as I have just argued, were indispensable in their function as bridgeheads of the colonial powers and hinges for the transfer of wealth to Europe is, of course, also economic performance, although not the one that is commonly assumed today). The project of colonialism was rapid exploitation, not development (not even dependent development, at least not in the first period of colonization). Colonialists considered their presence in the Latin American city as a time to acquire as much wealth as possible as quickly as possible in order to return with it to the Iberian Peninsula: "New World settlements were thus viewed, not as final destinations, but as temporary means for attainment of economic goals" (Portes 1977: 63). In economic terms such a strategy is called "rent seeking" – when income is accrued without corresponding labour input and consequently without productive output. Accordingly, the economies in the controlled territories developed only insofar as they met the need and greed of the Crown and of the local colonial masters. That production was aligned with the interests of the "mother countries" not only applied to mines and agriculture, but also to urban economies. Even if cities and their populations – i.e. the colonial bureaucracy, import-export merchants, workers and their respective families – were better off in the colonial division of labour than the indigenous population in mining towns or agricultural villages, it was also true that cities' economic structure was just as deformed, "impregnated" by the interests of the Crown, the Church, the powerful European merchants.

This had a profound impact on the social structure of the cities. Because trade between Europe and the viceroyalties was monopolized by the colonial powers (the merchants' guild of Mexico City, for example, held such a monopoly until 1795), an independent merchant elite comparable to European towns could not emerge in colonial cities. Artisanal activities and manufacturing were severely restricted, too. In order to protect the monopoly of producers on the Iberian Peninsula, who then could supply the "New World" with goods at inflated prices, manufacturing in colonial cities remained confined to low value-added and small-scale production to meet immediate needs of the population (such as cloth-making). Accordingly, the emergence of an industrial bourgeoisie was out of the question. In this way, external colonialism produced an internal social structure that corresponded to the condition of dependency. As Smith contends, "the interests and policies of urban elites must be placed in the context of their international class alliances. . . . urbanization is a political economic process hinging on explicit or implicit policymaking by societal elites who are tied to the international system in particular ways" (1996: 148). For the colonial city this meant that there were no conditions for a capitalist, i.e. an *accumulating* social stratum to emerge, a stratum that possessed money and sought to multiply it via investment and the exploitation of labour.

However, lacking dynamic actors with capitalist virtues – entrepreneurship, innovative, growth-oriented – the colonial cities could not become a generative force, not for themselves and even less for their regions or countries (Roberts 1978). These remained not only underperforming, but above all (and as a reason for their low performance) unintegrated. According to Amin (1974: 201f.), peripheral economies as those produced by colonialism are characterized by "structural features", of which the "disarticulation due to the adjustment of the orientation of production . . . to the needs of the center" is one of the most important, because it "prevents the transmission of the benefits of economic progress from the poles of development to the economy as a whole". Disarticulation means that nothing resembling a "national" economy ever came into being, but that different enclave

economies – the mines, export agriculture, the mostly self-sufficient haci-
enda, the larger cities dependent on European imports – emerged with
little or no interaction with each other (except those, of course, that served
to drain off surpluses). This social, economic and political fragmentation
"militated against the emergence of a stable network of towns and villages"
(Morse 1962: 479), whereas for the urban–rural relations it implied that not
even the form of uneven relationships that Adam Smith ([1776] 1977: 549)
had described for Europe ("... the commerce and manufactures of cities ...
have been the cause and occasion of the improvement and cultivation of the
country") emerged.

With formal political independence, little changed in all this. In Latin
America, import-substituting industrialization (an economic strategy that
restricted imports and sought to promote domestic production) was geographically concentrated in few cities. The imbalances created through
colonialism were thereby reinforced – the major cities continued to function as "suction pumps" (Timberlake 1987: 51) that soaked up the surplus
of producers in small towns and the countryside, however small it may
have been. Against this backdrop, in the 1960s Latin American academics
resumed the debate on internal colonialism, a concept that goes back to Russian and Italian Marxists who elaborated it to describe regional disparities
and the exploitation of peasants by city-dwellers. Departing from a conceptualization of colonialism as economic and political relations that ensured
the "domination and exploitation of *a total population (with its distinct
classes, proprietors, workers) by another population which also has distinct
classes (proprietors and workers)*", Mexican sociologist González Casanova
(1965: 33; emphasis added) suggested that Latin America's postcolonial realities were reminiscent of the colonial structure, which in turn "resembles
relations of domination and exploitation typical of the rural–urban structure of traditional society and of underdeveloped countries". In his view,
Latin American societies are societies of *internal* colonialism, because of
inter-regional relations of exploitation. These span the population of a country's "dominant centre" or "metropolis" and the rural (and, in the Mexican
case, indigenous) population. The city – and in the context of Latin America
in the 1950s and 1960s, this meant the capital city above all – is therefore not
only a locus of local exploitation (of workers by national or foreign entre-
preneurs in the industries), but also a proactive node in exploitation across
space, through asymmetrical relationships to producers in rural areas. For
the concept of internal colonialism, it is important to acknowledge that this
uneven development benefited not just the traditional few rich in the major
urban centres, but broader sections of the population there: merchants and
industrialists, employees of the state bureaucracy and in public services, and

to a certain extent even manufacturing workers (especially in state-owned enterprises).[25]

In sum, the literature referred to makes an essential difference between the generative city that developed in Europe (with the exception of Eastern Europe) in the late Middle Ages, and the "parasitic" (Hoselitz) or "predatory" (Portes) one that the Spanish and Portuguese colonial masters implanted in the conquered territories of Latin America. Yet, if we agree that cities in Latin America were "protagonist[s] in a large scheme of imperial colonization" (Morse 1962: 473), and if we reject any reification of the city (because cities do not act, they "only" create enabling or constraining conditions for actors), then we have to return to the question of whether and to what extent the three factors underlying the genius of cities – agglomeration, inter-city networks, the built environment – were addressed by the literatures discussed as facilitators of a city-based strategy of colonization. To be blunt, there is not too much on this – almost nothing on the importance of the built environment (except a brief hint in Frank [1969: 326] that in provincial towns the "store belonging to the large urban merchant became the new center of gravity of the region"), there is a little more on the role of agglomeration (i.e. density, diversity), and rather more on inter-city networks.

The literature reviewed in this section, with a focus on Latin America, addresses agglomeration less in terms of the positive economic externalities normally attributed to it and focuses more on the political benefits that result from the density of actors in cities. Friedmann (1973: 18f., 39), for example, drew attention to the fact that the geographical concentration of tangible and intangible resources in cities gave elites an edge over other actors. He particularly stressed that spatial proximity made the powerful more powerful. Referring to the period of inward-oriented development and import-substituting industrialization in Latin America (c.1945–80) he observed that "[p]oliticians, bureaucrats and businessmen mingle in exclusive social clubs and the city's top restaurants, send their children to private schools (or the national university), and form tight social networks of their own". Thereby, the "base of power is solidified within core regions" which allowed for political and economic control relations by which the dependency of rural areas and minor cities is secured. A case in point for the role played by mingling not in exclusive social clubs, but at the national university is the Faculty of Law of Mexico's state university UNAM, which can

---

25. Although there was no cross-referencing between literatures, the notions of "internal colonialism" and of the "aristocracy of labour" debates share common conceptual ground.

with good reason be considered a training ground for cadres until the late 1970s: "Flocking to the metropolis for law degrees which became their passports into the high bureaucracy, this new generation of politicians made the city their permanent residence, the locus of their entire careers, and the *prism that refracted their vision of the rest of the country*" (Kandell 1990: 487; emphasis added). Lipton (1977: 13, 62) argued similarly that, in addition to stressing that the main conflict in poorer countries is geographical in nature (rather than class-based or between different capital fractions), the specific spatial conditions of the city, namely density, decided who won the battle: "[U]rban classes have been able to 'win' most of the rounds of the struggle with the countryside", he claimed, because city-dwellers can develop, due to their physical and social closeness, common "interests, preferences, friends, places of residence and above all perceptions". For being more articulated than dispersed rural populations, city-dwellers can act jointly, as "threateners, promisers, lobbyists, dinner companions, flatterers, financiers and friends to senior administrators and politicians" (an idea we already know from Adam Smith).

The growing influence of the state after 1945 in the context of import-substituting industrialization strengthened the capital city in particular, because it made it opportune for private companies to locate close to the political decision-makers. For a certain period of time, state functionaries in Latin America took all relevant decisions in the economy, and resources were limited and therefore fought over. "As a consequence, managers are engaged in a constant dialogue with the government", describes Gilbert (1992: 56) the practice of the time. This "dialogue" included practices that were much easier to manage if one was on the spot: a business lunch here, an intervention there, maybe perhaps even an envelope of money or a threat behind closed doors.

The representatives of the "internal colonialism" argument add another contention. González Casanova (1965) claims that the ability of the "national" elites to impose colonial relationships within the country comes from a monopolistic control over typical urban economic activities such as trade, communication and credit. This applied to the respective capital cities, where both the banking system and the rich and their money were centralized, but not exclusively. In Mexico, for example, Ladino merchants in provincial towns continued to enjoy both monopolistic and monopsonistic advantages in trade relations with the predominantly Indigenous people in their respective hinterlands even during the period of economic modernization during import substitution. At the local markets in their town, they could set prices for the goods they sold (because the indigenous population was too immobile to move to another market), but also for the products they bought from the peasants, for which they were the only buyers. Rodolfo Stavenhagen (2013: 19) points out that for the latter case – the monopsonistic control of goods bought from the Indigenous peoples – a cultural monopoly also played a role. The economic power of the urban Ladino merchants "is reinforced by their cultural superiority as expressed by their knowledge of price-building mechanisms, of the laws of the country; above all, of the Spanish language, which, being unknown to the Indians, represents one more factor of inferiority and social oppression".

On the subject of inter-city networks, we have already seen the argument that the colonization of Latin America was organized through a city system. Frank (1969: 6) claimed that the development of underdevelopment in the colonial period as well as afterwards was managed through "a whole chain of constellations of metropoles and satellites [which] relates all parts of the whole system from its metropolitan center in Europe or the United States to the farthest outpost in the Latin American countryside". This notion is actually based on textbook knowledge in urban and regional planning in the 1950s and 1960s, *but turned on its head.* In the planning literature, the need for a well-developed city system (or, as it was often called, an urban hierarchy) for efficient development processes was emphasized, with "well-developed" meaning reasonably well-balanced (in terms of population size, but also as regards productive facilities such as industries, communication and other infrastructures). The larger cities were seen as growth poles, from which economic development was thought to "trickle down" the hierarchy of cities and spread across the country. Accordingly, a balanced hierarchy of cities was attributed the role of being the backbone of the national economy, the means to organize and integrate the social and economic space of a country and to diffuse innovation and economic growth.

Noticing the persistence and even deepening of regional inequalities, John Friedmann was one of the first to abandon the optimistic notion that a balanced inter-city network would aid the diffusion of innovation and economic growth. Rather, the urban hierarchy (balanced or not) could work in exactly the opposite way, as a "structure of authority–dependency relations" in which a "hierarchy of urban centres [is] exercising control over both national and regional economies" (Friedmann 1967: 18; 1973: 26). In such cases, cities' external relations were neither of mutual advantage nor benefiting the rest of the country, but rather embodying the organizational framework for uneven development which at some point becomes even "dysfunctional" (Friedmann 1967: 33) for a country's general economic development. The core idea behind this critical turn in the analysis of city networks is to understand them as one layer in an asymmetrical division of labour. In this perspective, two questions arise: which city specializes (or can specialize) in which activities (high value or low value, to put it bluntly), and how, in whose favour, are the created values distributed? In itself, the existence of a inter-city network does not indicate what the relationships are like between its nodes – the "stations" of a division of labour. They can be structured in a complementary way, to common benefit, or be one-sided and exploitative. In the latter case, the inter-city network would turn into a means of core areas to siphon off and appropriate surpluses from the peripheries. As Frank's quote above has already indicated, it is true for almost all nodes in this uneven network that they are exploited "from above" (from the next node closer to the centre), while they themselves exploit "downwards" (towards the next node closer to the periphery). "From this point of view", Roberts contends, there is a

> chain of exploitative relationships that link the metropolitan country to the major city and dominant classes of the dependent country [and that] extends from these classes to traders and producers located in provincial towns, right down to the peasant producer or to the landless rural worker. . . . At each stage of appropriation or expropriation there must always be a class of people who derive advantage from their situation and are prepared to act as agents in channelling the local resources to the metropolis. (Roberts 1978: 14)

This was the case in the colonial period, where "the urban hierarchy" created "fitted into a larger imperial calculus of political and fiscal privilege" (Morse 1971: 6), and it also applies to the period since independence. Referring to Mexico, González Casanova and Frank provide examples of towns at the lower end of the exploitation chain that, unknown as they may be, are nodes in the global transfer of wealth. While González Casanova (1965: 34) refers to Zacapoaxtla, a town in the state of Puebla, which in the 1960s had some 20,000 inhabitants, as being involved in the organization of relations of "interchange plainly unfavorable to the Indian communities" (*ibid.*), Frank (1969: 325) names Tlaxiaco, a town in the state of Oaxaca, which had even fewer inhabitants. Nevertheless it "extracted in parasite fashion" profit from the surrounding villages through the same means deployed by the national capital (but on a smaller scale): monopolistic control of the distribution of urban goods and in communication, monopsonistic control of the sales of goods produced by the indigenous population. In both cases, the unevenness of the division of labour and of the urban network corresponded to a racialized hierarchy: the higher up in the hierarchy a city was, the whiter, more European it was, the lower down, the more Indigenous. In this sense, "[t]he urban hierarchy of city and village . . . preserved and *enforced* status distinctions between categories of the population" (Roberts 1978: 37; emphasis added).

In this chapter I have presented different accounts of the role of cities in the production of uneven development. While one intention was to show the basis on which my notion of the Janus-facedness of the genius of cities is built, the historical and geographical breadth of the cases the various authors refer to aimed to underpin that this Janus-facedness is a generic process, a characteristic that cities across time and space share. Taking the reviewed literatures together, they cover a period of six centuries, and even if their geographical focus is not equally broad, at least two major areas of the world are examined in depth (Europe, Latin America). Other regions also find their way in, especially through Braudel. In sum the chapter provides sufficient examples of how agglomeration economies, embeddedness in inter-city networks and the massiveness of the built environment have been the basis for urban elites in different regions and at different times to achieve control over people in other regions. Trusting that this literature review will be convincing as to why cities should be conceived of as an analytical category in thinking about exploitation and misery, as an *explanans* that helps us better understand uneven development, in the next chapter I seek to demonstrate how the thoughts discussed so far can be recovered and made fruitful for today's analyses of uneven development.

CHAPTER 5

TOWARDS A CITIFIED RESEARCH AGENDA FOR UNEVEN DEVELOPMENT

For the purpose of this chapter, namely to indicate what research on the Janus-facedness of cities might look like, it is once again helpful to consult Braudel. Although he writes about capitalism from the fifteenth to the eighteenth century, his work offers more than just insights into history. Braudel provides us with a method for a citified analysis of capitalism, a way of doing research in order to gain new insights into the functioning of uneven development. He draws our attention to the various "weapons of domination" which, in all their diversity, have two things in common: first, they all come from cities, are invented and produced there and orchestrated from there. Second, they all serve the economic interests of the dominant groups there (in the times that Braudel writes about, basically long-distance traders); their goal is to make value or surplus that people have produced wherever to "flow" into their city. Yet, Braudel (1984: 248) also urges us to pay attention not only to the cities themselves, but in particular to their networks: "It is with these connections, meeting-points and multiple links that we shall be particularly concerned, since they reveal the way in which a dominant economy can exploit subordinate economies". At each node of the inter-city networks, there are different ways in which the appropriation of surplus is organized, according to the requirements of geographic or historical circumstances, and each way requires specific weapons. Braudel accordingly enumerates different types, namely "shipping, trade, industry, credit, and political power or violence", each of them with its particular value (1984: 35). There is, however, one weapon that Braudel does not mention here, but which, as we have seen, he discusses at length elsewhere, namely the physical infrastructure of cities. Following on from this, in this chapter I use three examples to show how we can locate the production of uneven development in cities, first by looking at particular buildings, and second by scrutinizing particular capitalist practices (namely super-exploitation and monopoly formation) and the actors who exercise them, and what they have to do with the genius of cities.

THE BUILT ENVIRONMENT AS RESULT AND
MEANS OF CAPITALIST EXPLOITATION

A first example of how cities' proactive role in networks of exploitation can be scrutinized starts from precisely this, from the built environment. We have learned that Braudel attributes a very prominent role to Amsterdam's warehouses, which he describes as a key weapon of the city's merchants in their quest to make themselves and their city the centre of the expanding capitalist world-system. Many of these warehouses are part of a new "port city", built in the late sixteenth and early seventeenth centuries, which is now designated a World Heritage Site that UNESCO describes as "of exceptional value to humanity".[26] For all the beauty of the buildings and the urban enviroment they help to create, to ascribe the Canal Ring Area exceptional value to humanity *as a whole* is, of course, highly Eurocentric, comprehensible only from the perspective of the profiteers of the triumphant march of capitalism, of the city-driven capitalism, as Braudel says. "The Wretched Of The Earth" (Fanon 2005), the victims of the ingenuity of Amsterdam and its merchants, peasants in Poland and miners in Mexico and Peru, but also the bourgeoisie in those countries that did not come into being thanks to the practices of Amsterdam's merchants, would probably object (Moore 2010a, 2010b; Robins 2011).

Many of the buildings that UNESCO certifies as being of exceptional value to humanity are both the result and the means of capitalist exploitation. Result, because their construction required considerable resources, and means because the buildings themselves served as "weapons" to appropriate these resources. Take, for example, Hamburg, the city where I live. Here, the Speicherstadt and the Kontorhaus District are also World Heritage Sites because, as UNESCO puts it, they exemplify "the effects of the rapid growth in international trade in the late 19th and early 20th centuries". Another view of Speicherstadt, one less dazzled by its architectural brilliance, would acknowledge that it was born out of the German *Reichsgründung* and the associated imperial aspirations, and that it was a heart of German colonialism, serving Hamburg merchants as a warehouse for rubber, palm oil, cocoa

---

26. See https://whc.unesco.org/en/about/.

beans, ivory, coffee, cinnamon, bananas and tea. Using the World Heritage list as a guide, the study of the proactive role of cities' built environment in exploitation can easily continue. In Vienna, the city where I have spent most of my life, the historic centre with its Baroque buildings, monuments and gardens is another World Heritage Site (although in 2017 UNESCO placed it on the World Heritage in Danger list, because of a high-rise real estate project). Here, too, the city's apparent wealth is based on uneven development and exploitation across space, with the difference only that it was internal colonialism, wealth siphoned off from the inner peripheries of the Austro-Hungarian Empire which made the monumental architecture possible. Finally, in Mexico City, my third home, the historic centre, also on the UNESCO list, was built by the Spanish conquerers and served as the site from where they subjugated and controlled the people and territories that became the Viceroyalty of New Spain. What Portes (1977: 64) says about cities in colonial Latin America in general applies to Mexico City in particular, namely that they were of a "predatory nature . . . closely linked with the interests of both the central governments and the colonists themselves".[27]

The fact that UNESCO shines its spotlight on all this history of exploitation cast in stone repeatedly leads to protests (such things shouldn't be considered "of exceptional value to humanity"), but, surprisingly, it does not prompt us to correct our overly positive image of cities. In German, the word for "monument" is *Denkmal*, which, with a little wordplay, can be transformed into "denk-mal", which literally means "think (about it)". Cities do us the favour of showcasing and storing accumulated wealth (which in cities has always been more than the wealth of the very few very rich) through their built environments, even though the time may be past when the wealth was forcefully appropriated from other people. While the misery created in the course of this wealth production is in most cases not immediately visible, it is detectable. Cities are windows of opportunity for critical research, not in the temporal sense (a period of time during which action can be taken), but in the geographical sense: cities have numerous buildings, places, streets, etc., that invite us to search for the exploitation that lies behind their discernible wealth. Cities, thus, provide food for thought. If we seize it, then we could reach a more comprehensive understanding of them, by sheding light on their bright *and* dark sides, the relationships between the two, and, most importantly, "what analysis of one brings to the other" (Phelps *et al.* 2018:

---

27. It is, however, fair to say that Mexico City also has World Heritage sites that don't have this exploitative character, or at least not so bluntly, such as UNAM, the largest university in Latin America, and the Gardens of Xochimilco.

237). For urban studies and the ongoing debate on how to theorize cities, that would be a big win.

SUPER-EXPLOITATION AND SUPER-PROFITS

Let us now return to Braudel's weapons of exploitation more generally. Theories of uneven development provide us with information on key mechanisms, and we have already become acquainted with the two fundamentally different approaches. Proponents of the "differentiated growth model" see in regionally differentiated growth dynamics the main reason for uneven development, while connectivity-based explanations focus on value or surplus transfers across space: what is produced by people in one locality or region is being appropriated and used by actors outside the regions. In addition, two different foci can be distinguished in connectivity-based explanations. The first draws attention to the sphere of production, the area in which surplus value (in the Marxian sense) is created and appropriated by the owners of capital by extracting unpaid labour time from workers. The second centres interest in the sphere of circulation, in trade, where appropriated surplus value is distributed among different capitalists and also regionally. Since both spheres are elementary for the functioning of accumulation, the two foci of exploitation do not compete with each other, let alone exclude each other. Rather, they complement each other.

As for the sphere of production, Marx pointed out two ways in which surplus value can be increased: by the extension of the working day, or by shortening the labour time necessary to manufacture a product (i.e., productivity increases). The appropriation of surplus value thus ultimately depends on the effective squeezing of wages, relative to labour time and/or to the quantity of goods produced. One of the most important of the relational theories of uneven development, that of unequal exchange (Emmanuel 1972; Amin 1976), focuses on just that. At first glance, unequal exchange theory seems to place asymmetric *trade relations* between countries at the centre of its explanation for the emergence of global inequalities. Building on the Prebisch–Singer thesis (Prebisch 1950; Singer 1950), which sees in the secular deterioration of the terms of trade[28] the main reason of what

---

28. The terms of trade is a measure of the prices of the products a country or region exports relative to the prices of the products it imports. In other words, they indicate how much a country or region can pay for imports with its exports. The terms of trade deteriorate when exports become cheaper relative to imports, i.e. when less can be bought with export revenues.

then was called "underdevelopment", Marxist economist Arghiri Emmanuel (1972) contended that unequal exchange not only happens between different sectors of the economy, as analyzed by Marx, but also between *countries*. The rationale for his claim is that rates of surplus value differ not only between sectors, as contended by Marx, but also between countries, because wages differ between them. However, and this is crucial, Emmanuel and other theorists of unequal exchange argued that these wage differentials between countries do not stem from corresponding productivity differences. Against the mainstream position of their time (which, by the way, is still held today), they claimed that wage differentials exist even though the countries' economies have equal – or at least similar – levels of productivity. In such a situation, trade between countries becomes unequal because goods are exchanged from a country where "labor of the same productivity is rewarded at a lower rate" (Amin 1976: 149) than in the other country involved in the trade. Consequently, the first country must expend more quanta of labour than it receives in exchange.

If wage differences between countries are not the result of productivity differences, they must have extra-economic causes. The key contention of the proponents of unequal exchange theory (and of dependency theorists alike) is that wages in peripheral countries are *politically* fixed, and that is, kept lower than economic productivity would permit. Being dominated and exploited by the centre of the world economy, the elites of peripheral countries, who themselves also want to profit from exploitation, are "forced" to depress wages so that they also get a piece of the pie. It is therefore political interventions which cause the depression of wages in peripheral countries and which allow the expansion of surplus value production to an extent that domestic elites still make their profits even though there is a massive surplus drain towards core countries.

This contention underlies the theory of super-exploitation, a concept that was popularized by Ruy Mauro Marini (1973), Brazilian economist and sociologist, and one of the key proponents of dependency theory. He argued that the enormous wage differentials between rich and poor countries are due to differences in the rate of workers' exploitation,[29] which is higher in Latin America than in core countries. In fact, the rate of exploitation there is so high that the wages paid lie below workers' social reproduction costs, a situation Marini calls "super-exploitation". Current debates on the new

---

29. The rate of exploitation is defined as the rate between the time a worker takes to create value equal to what he or she consumes and the time he or she produces surplus value for the capitalist.

imperialism of the twenty-first century (Smith 2016; Suwandi 2019) draw on this concept, arguing that "globalization", i.e. the extension and geographical dispersion of commodity chains since the 1980s, is driven by the quest to extract additional profits from the super-exploitation of workers in the peripheries (Selwyn 2019). Accordingly, capital accumulation has increasingly become a truly global concern, with the consequence, among others, that "class is a world-historical totality constituted through multiple scales" (Campling *et al.* 2016: 1749).

Labour arbitrage, a practice of companies to take advantage of lower labour costs elswhere, either by outsourcing production there, or by importing cheap labour via immigration, has become a common capitalist strategy. It is not for nothing that the countries that are involved in this practice on the "lower" end of the transaction are referred to as "low-wage countries". While this term may sound despicable, it corresponds to reality. The *raison d'être* of countries that have experienced rapid export-oriented industrialization in recent decades is that they provide the reservoir of so-called cheap labour required for this form of exploitation. The real wage gap[30] between the new industrial sites in the peripheries and the traditional core countries is huge (although often difficult to calculate, as comparable productivity data are scarce). To give an impression, one example will suffice. The share of employee compensation in the gross value added in industry (2000–20) is more than a quarter lower in Poland than in neighbouring Germany, while in Mexico it is as much as 30 per cent lower than in the United States (OECD 2022). Because manufacturing workers in Poland or Mexico mostly produce for the world market, in companies that are firmly integrated into global commodity chains, this wage gap allows the corporations that control the respective commodity chains to make extra profits.

Importantly, these wage gaps do not come out of nowhere: many of the economies to which production has been relocated in recent decades are characterized by poor or extremely poor working conditions and a lack of political rights, such as the right to organize, according to the International Trade Union Confederation (ITUC 2022). While in Asia corporations seek to prevent bargaining power of workers from emerging (Suwandi 2019), in Latin America corporate practices have eroded it (Bensusán & Middlebrook 2012). One means of achieving this is the promotion of subcontracting in manufacturing, which allows workers to be hired in subsidiaries or sub-subsidiaries on less favourable terms than in the parent company. When Brazil, for example, approved such an expansion of outsourcing in 2017, it was hailed

---

30. Hourly labour cost per employee, adjusted for productivity.

by *Latin American Lawyer*, a digital magazine of leading law firms directed at their multinational clients in Latin America, as "a boost to business" that "provide[s] a fresh element in labour relations . . . to increase market efficiency and adapt to a modern economy".[31] As a result of anti-labour policies, Brazil, Bangladesh and the Philippines are worldwide among the ten worst countries for working people, while China, India and Indoensia are attested by the ITUC (2022) as countries where workers' rights are not guaranteed at all; in Vietnam and in Mexico, two other principal outsourcing countries, regular and systematic violations of these rights are the order of the day. This denial of the most fundamental rights for workers makes it possible to depress wages, even below the level of a so-called living wage, i.e. a remuneration that allows workers to afford a decent standard of living for themselves and their families. Globalization is, thus, built on super-exploitation.

This super-exploitation stems from a deliberate corporate agency. For their anti-labour policies, corporations have various weapons in their arsenals. Direct violence is one of them, always has been and will be. But beyond brute force there are other, more sophisticated methods to exacerbate labour exploitation. Some of these methods are illegal and thus their use is made possible by weak enforcement of laws. But other methods exist where the boundaries between legal and illegal are blurred, or are legal in the sense that they are enshrined in and protected by national employment and labour laws, trade treaties or international agreements. One example of this legitimization of super-exploitation is the promotion of subcontracting already discussed. Another example comes from the transport industry in the European Union: according to the German Federal Office for Logistics and Mobility (Bundesamtes für Logitik und Mobilität 2023; data for 2022), more than one third of the kilometres driven on roads in Germany by trucks were by drivers whose trucks were registered in an Eastern European EU country (with Poland having the highest share, 18.6 per cent, which has been rising steadily for years). This is good business for the freight carriers: under Polish law, a truck driver receives about €9 per hour, but €22 according to German law. Drivers who earn the Polish wage (and who often do not come from Poland, but from the Philippines, Uzbekistan, Kazakhstan or Tajikistan) nevertheless have to pay the same price for the rest-stop services of German highways as the German drivers – they are, in a word, super-exploited workers within the EU and its legislation.

Legal anti-labour policies that seek to prepare the ground for the practice

---

31. See https://thelatinamericanlawyer.com/brazilian-employment-reform-a-boost-to-business/.

of super-exploitation culminate in so-called union avoidance initiatives, which aim at disrupting or preventing the formation of unions or their attempts to increase their membership in a workplace. In the last decades, a veritable union-busting industry has developed, first and most strongly in the United States. Law firms there are at its forefront. Theirs is the business of "defeating union organizing campaigns and keeping their clients . . . union free. These [law] firms have perfected union avoidance techniques that make it extraordinarily difficult for unions to organize in the private sector" (Logan 2020: 77).

To give a sense of this union busting industry, take a look at the Barnes & Thornburg LLP website. This law firm is not particularly large in a relative sense. With 658 attorneys in the US and a gross revenue of over $600 million in 2022, it is only the 76th largest law firm in the US (and the 103rd largest in the world[32]), although the six-fold increase in revenues over the past 20 years is striking. Its blatant sales pitch is, however, remarkable. "A union flyer was posted on one of your facility's employee bulletin board last night. What should you do next", asks Barnes & Thornburg LLP, addressing potential clients:

> Fortunately, you don't have to know the answer – because we do. We have the experience, depth and understanding to deal with any situation at a moment's notice. We will get you through this – our professionals have worked with employers from coast-to-coast, across most industries and with most of the major unions. Our passion is to preserve a client's freedom to manage and to assist our clients in helping them remain union-free. Our goal is to engage clients in union avoidance activities prior to an actual campaign – to avoid campaigns altogether. . . . We estimate our team has helped manage hundreds of union organizing attempts and/or campaigns, and our clients have obtained favorable results in more than 96% of the campaigns in which we have been involved.[33]

Law firms that offer anti-union services, like Barnes & Thornburg, have not only grown in number, but they have taken their tactics beyond the United States. Just like many other law firms, accountancy firms, tax

---

32. See   https://www.law.com/law-firm-profile/?id=25&name=Barnes-&-Thornburg-LLP&slreturn=20230519090331

33. See https://btlaw.com/work/practices/labor-and-employment/union-avoidance.

advisors and financial institutions, they are among the business service firms that have globalized over the past decades in order to assist their clients in starting and running businesses abroad. The proliferation of law firms specializing in anti-union services is helping to establish a "New Union Avoidance Internationalism" (Logan 2020: 80) that poses a significant threat to workers, both locally, in specific factories and export processing zones, and more generally, on a global stage, to counter international campaigns for worldwide labour standards compliance.

A case in point is Littler Mendelson, the world's largest law firm specializing in labour law representing the employers' side. A local San Francisco firm until the 1990s, Littler Mendelson expanded first throughout the United States via mergers and acquisitions, and then, starting in 2010, internationally. Today, the firm has 47 offices outside the US in 26 countries, nearly 40 per cent of them in Latin America. Littler Mendelson reveals little about its clients, but in Latin America they include (directly or through partner offices) General Motors, Novartis AG and Uber. In Mexico, for example, Littler has three offices, located in the capital and in two of the country's most important industrial centres, Saltillo (a centre of the automotive industry) and Monterrrey (home to CEMEX and other building materials and beer industries). With 26 shareholders and associates, Littler is relatively small compared to the large US law firms in Mexico, but this should be put into perspective given that the firm is dedicated exclusively to representing management in labour and employment matters. The spirit in which this representation of corporations is undertaken is made unambiguously clear by Jorge Sales Boyoli, who, until summer 2023, was partner in Littler Mexico. He laments that "while US labor law generally focuses on how to efficiently (and legally) operate a profitable business, Mexican labour law generally focuses on worker rights" (Roth & Sales Boyoli 2021; own translation). His legal advice to large Mexican and global companies in collective bargaining or strikes against some of Mexico's largest unions aims to ensure that worker-friendly labour laws do not cause his clients to lose the comparative advantage they currently have by producing in Mexico, namely "low wages and a unionism [which is] in not a few cases, inactive" (*ibid.*). That the renegotiation of the NAFTA agreement in 2017–18 forced by then-US President Donald Trump and the presidency of the leftist Andrés Manuel López Obrador in Mexico have made times harder for company unions (*sindicatos blancos*) "hurts deeply", he complains (quoted in Callejas 2021; own translation).

Before addressing what the anti-union activities of law firms like Littler Mendelson have to do with the genius of cities, I turn to another central practice in the production of uneven development, the formation of monopolies.

MONOPOLIES AND THE GEOGRAPHICAL TRANSFER OF SURPLUS

I return once again to theories of uneven development and their explanations of its causes. In addition to the focus on the sphere of production, attention is drawn to circulation. Capitalist actors struggle over the distribution of surplus value created in production between themselves and between different regions, and exchange relations are a field of this struggle. However, the fact that trade is "only" about the social and geographical distribution (or redistribution) of surplus value and not about its production does not make it a secondary arena for the issue of uneven development: the question of who can ultimately dispose of the appropriated surplus, i.e. who can use it for investment, determines accumulation dynamics. Accordingly, economic development becomes uneven among other things because of asymmetric exchange relations in which capital for investment is redistributed, socially and geographically. Hadjimichalis (1984) has theorized such redistribution and centralization of capital as a "geographical transfer of value" which occurs when "value produced for exchange by workers at one locality: (a) is realized by the capitalists who have employed these workers, but profits have been reinvested elsewhere; and/or (b) is at least partially realized by the capitalists who have employed these workers and is added as excess profits to other capitalists in other localities" (*ibid.*: 338).

How is this geographical transfer of value (or surplus, in world-systems conceptualization) achieved? Hadjimichalis (1984) names direct methods, ranging from brute force to profit repatriation, and indirect ones, which work through market mechanisms. However, and this is the key point, one must not think of this "market" as a textbook market where supply and demand meet to form prices freely. Rather, really existing capitalist markets are far from this ideal. Firstly, a considerable part of trade does not take place *between* firms, but actually *within* them, as so-called intra-firm or related-party trade (for the US, for example, transactions within corporate structures account for more than 40 per cent of all foreign trade [U.S. Census Bureau 2022]). Accordingly, corporations have many possibilities to manipulate the "market" prices of the traded goods (something referred to as "transfer-pricing"), for example so that as little tax as possible is incurred. Really existing markets are distorted by a second method which is, according to the theorists of world-systems analysis, the central cause of the unequal distribution of surpluses along commodity chains and hence of uneven development. I have already said that capitalists strive for monopolies or quasi-monopolies because they generate easier and higher profits than market competition. As a consequence,

[t]he total surplus extracted in these commodity chains was at no point in time distributed evenly in terms of the geographical location of the creation of the surplus, but was always concentrated to a disproportionate degree in some zones rather than in others. . . . The basic logic is that the accumulated surplus is distributed unequally in favor of those able to achieve various kinds of temporary monopolies in the market networks. This is a 'capitalist' logic. (Wallerstein 1991: 109, 247)

Because in the circulation sphere surpluses are reallocated, but not multiplied, the extra profits achieved through monopolies (essentially established by the big capitalists, namely transnational corporations) go at the expense of the profits of producers who are either less protected from competition or not protected at all. Accordingly, monopolies lead to a "hierarchization of space . . . an ever greater polarization between the core and peripheral zones of the world-economy, not only in terms of distributive criteria (real income levels, quality of life) but even more importantly in the loci of the accumulation of capital" (Wallerstein 1983: 30). Monopolies lead thus to uneven development, just as super-exploitation does.

Yet, how can capitalists achieve monopoly positions? The tried and tested means are barriers to entry. Some of them may be geographic (e.g., availability of raw materials), others may result from the characteristics of the production process itself (e.g., economies of scale), but most of them are deliberately designed and implemented: licensing, product and labour standards, import restrictions, and, most importantly, patents. Patents serve "very, very clearly . . . to crowd out a competitor", says the managing partner of a global law firm in Hamburg in interview (quoted in Parnreiter 2019: 88), and "to have a monopoly would always be suitable". Patents are, thus, another weapon in exploitation and appropriation of surplus.

Establishing – and defending – monopolies requires the backing of an effective national and, increasingly, supranational legal system, albeit one that is nationally-backed. Patents are granted by national patent offices or their regional counterparts such as the European Patent Office, and they are enforced in court, again in national (and in rarer cases supranational) institutions. However, the legal system must be functional not only technically, but also politically: it must be able to defend the interests of its "own" capitalists *against* potential competitors. In sum, just as the practice of transnational corporations to super-exploit workers in peripheral countries is enabled and protected by political interventions in the labour market (for example, through specific labour laws, regulations on union [non]activity, etc.), the extra profits derived from monopolies are also the result of political intervention. "What are the services that capitalists need of the state?" asks Wallerstein (1999: 63), at the same time providing the answer: "The first and greatest service they require is protection against the free market".

In addition to state power, establishing monopolies requires professionals who can devise the big strategies and do the day-to-day legwork to implement them. These are lawyers specializing in intellectual property rights. Their advice is becoming increasingly important and has even become indispensable in many cases, for several reasons. The economy has become both more knowledge-intensive and more globalized since the 1980s, both of which have contributed to a decline in the importance of traditional geographic (i.e., nation-state administered) barriers to entry (such as tariffs and import restrictions). Companies consequently try to minimize inter-firm rivalry through other measures, among the most important of which is the protection of intangible assets such as knowledge or brands.[34] Accordingly, the number of patent applications has skyrocketed, with a sixfold increase in the number of worldwide annual applications between 1980 and 2020 (from 530,000 to 3.4 million) (World Intellectual Property Organization 2023). In accordance with the uneven geographies of economic dynamics and state power, the distribution of patent applications is geographically uneven. In 2020, 90 per cent of all applications came from China, the USA, Japan, South Korea and the European Union. What is more important for the purpose of this book, however, is the high geographical concentration of patenting by the location of the law firm that represented the applicant. Almost a third of the more than 112,000 patents granted by the European Patent Office in 2020 (so-called B1 patents) were given to companies represented by law firms in London (16.2 per cent) and Munich (14 per cent), making these two cities the undisputed IP capitals of Europe – Berlin, the city with the third most granted patents, filed only 3 per cent, whereas Paris filed 2.6 per cent (Kluwer Law International 2021).

WHY ANTI-LABOUR AND INTELLECTUAL PROPERTY LAWYERS DEPEND ON URBAN CONTEXTS

After having identified weapons for enforcing uneven development, namely anti-labour policies and patenting, we can return to Braudel's call to use the

---

34. In addition to patents, trademarks and copyright are important in obtaining monopolies.

focus on cities and their networks to study how exploitation – as a daily practice – works. In the two cases presented, law firms are central actors in the weapon-making processes. To be sure, the biggest profiteers of the extra profits achieved through workers' super-exploitation and by monopolies are transnational corporations, which therefore can be considered to be the driving forces behind the strategies outlined. I also mentioned that state involvement is essential in both cases: states provide their apparatus for the implementation and enforcement of labour-hostile legislation and for laws securing the protection of intellectual property. However, in my examples I have also pointed to experts, professionals specializing in particular types of knowledge and experiences necessary to produce and maintain uneven development: corporate labour lawyers, who interpret the law in a pro-business sense and then seek to establish such an interpretation as universally accepted and who lobby policy-makers for anti-labour legislation, and intellectual property lawyers who make sure that aspirant, often smaller and in most cases "foreign" companies are denied, or at least hindered or delayed, entry into their clients' market. We have already seen that patent lawyers are highly concentrated in a few cities. The same is true, albeit not to the same extreme, of the anti-labour law firms. Of course, this is not by accident.

Services such as those provided by the law firms referred to require very specific conditions, because they are typically knowledge-intensive, and their product is not standardized, but tailored to a customer's needs. Therefore law firms and other business services – in addition to legal services, they encompass financial, insurance and real estate advice, as well as business consulting – cluster in dense, "buzzing" learning-inducing and technology-enabled environments. Such settings are not ubiquitously available; they only exist highly selectively, in very specific cities – the global cities (Sassen 1991; Taylor 2004; Parnreiter 2019; Meeteren & Kleibert 2022). Therefore, and that is one of the core arguments of the respective literature, business services are "intrinsically urban in character" (Scott & Storper 2015: 9). For my reflections about the Janus-faced nature of the genius of cities, this means that the professional advice that establishes anti-labour policies or monopolies is also intrinsically urban in character.

The strategic and material means of direct use of violence do not necessarily have to be urban in origin – just think of the brute force that underlay "super-exploitation" in feudal relations of production, or that with which the transnational corporations of today's drug economy enforce their monopsonies and monopolies. Things are different, however, when it comes to the more sophisticated methods of exploitation and surplus appropriation, those in which the brutality is hidden behind a veneer of the rule of law (for example, when countries set legal minimum wages that are not sufficient for survival, let alone a dignified life), or which are designed in such a way as to make the relations of exploitation opaque (e.g., through chains of subcontracting in manufacturing that are almost impossible to track). These more advanced methods of exploitation tend not to be conceived and developed by the coroporations' headquarters or by policy-makers. The weapons with which the anti-labour struggles are waged and monopolies are erected and defended come from the arsenals of external consulting firms, forged by top lawyers, assisted where necessary by investment bankers, tax advisors, strategic business planners, etc. They are all very creative in what they do – just as the investment bankers and financial institutions have been who devised and put into practice the system of subprime mortgages. This system, let us remember, which was designed to trap poor, primarily African-American and Latino households in the US in debt, made some investment bankers and financial institutions very rich, but robbed millions of people of their homes when it collapsed like a house of cards in 2007–08. Critically, the instruments of the subprime system – the collateralized debt obligations, above all – are, as Mould (2016: 159; emphasis added) aptly put it, "the *very products that this creativity and innovation* [i.e. of cities] bring about". The financial industry, as well as the top lawyers and tax advisors who make tax evasion possible and who help defraud states (i.e., the general public) of millions upon millions of dollars and euros (as documented by the yearly reports of the *Tax Justice Network*) – all of them and many more depend on cities' creative potential to successfully do their business of making the rich richer. That implies that cities' external relations to other cities, the material and immaterial flows that underlie inter-city networks, are typically not horizontal, as is usually claimed in the literature (see Chapter 3), but, in contrast, are usually asymmetrical, creating, maintaining and reinforcing relations of exploitation.

What cities and their networks offer lawyers and other business service firms has been explored by some work in the context of global city research (e.g. Parnreiter 2019; Bassens *et al.* 2021), but how exactly agglomeration, embeddedness in networks, and the built environment feed exploitative practices remains an open field of research. Even in the social scientific study of law, where scholars point out that law, like power, is spatially constituted, for which reason the "where" of law matters for the way it is practised (Braverman *et al.* 2014), references to the city as a specific space are rare. Many of the respective studies suffer from the limitation of methodological nationalism. This can be seen, for example, in assessments critical of the *Anglo-American* bias of many business-related areas of law, while a Manhattan-, Loop- or The City-bias has not been noticed (let alone criticized). References to New

York, Chicago or London would, however, be much more accurate, because Anglo-American dominance is primarily produced in these (and a handful of other) cities, and not in the UK or the USA as territorial states. Even where the outstanding importance in research and teaching of elite universities such as Cambridge, Harvard or the Sorbonne is brought into focus (e.g. Roberts 2017), the urban, i.e. its very peculiar properties, is not dealt with as an analytical category in examining the writing and speaking of law. Helmut Aust and Janne Nijman (2021: 7) therefore contend, with reference to international law scholarship, that "[f]or most of the twentieth- as well as early-twenty-first-century . . . it is apt to speak of an 'invisibility' of cities". While matters look different when it comes to work on legal geographies in the context of the development of international financial centres (e.g. Wójcik 2013; van Meeteren & Bassens 2016), where an appreciation of cities' roles in uneven development mechanisms is enhanced, and while the now highly visible presence of cities on the international stage (through networks such as United Cities and Local Governments or Cities Alliance which are advocating for local political and economic interests of cities) has encouraged reflection on the relationship between law and cities, much work remains to be be done in this respect.

An example of how this could be done is given by Daniel Litwin (2021: 430f., 434, 441; emphasis added), who calls for greater awareness of how the "urban situation" impacts on the "practices, representations, and epistemologies" of lawyers specializing in international law. Building on the social science finding that the production of knowledge is always located in a specific socio-spatial context, by which knowledge is accordingly shaped, Litwin stresses that for international law scholarship this shared context is the *city*. Lawyers' practices – both their daily routine and the more exceptional cases of treaty negotiations or international disputes – take place in cities' social and material settings. Accordingly, lawyers' "engagement with international law is principally expressed and mediated through concrete experiences within the urban". This has consequences, both for the law itself and the way it is practised. The "urban situation . . . informs a *particular* view of the world", whereby this particularity of the worldview refers not only to the urban in general, but to the fact that the "community of practice" of international lawyers (like those of other sub-disciplines of law, such as labour law or intellectual proerty) is not formed in any cities, but in global cities, predominantly those in the Global North (for the international law scholarship Geneva, New York City, The Hague and Washington, DC stand out). Moreover, the urban experience that these elite lawyers have and that shapes their professional practice is a very peculiar one. They live and work in highly segregated, privileged neighbourhoods of global cities that not only have nothing to do with the experiences of the world's population, but also nothing to do with those of the majority of the residents of these cities. Accordingly, when speaking of the formative influence of cities on legal thinking and practices, one must add that, "from a socio-legal perspective", international law must, regardless of its claim to be universal, "be understood as a mostly urban core phenomenon" (more precisely still: a phenomenon of a very elite version of the "urban"). What results is a "structural bias" – "international lawyers may be universalizing a point of view informed by . . . [their] urban situation". "International law is what cities do and how they think", says Litwin provocatively, and suggests that for this reason it might probably be no coincidence that Global Administrative Law emerged "within the plutocratic and global city of New York".

A preferred lens through which Litwin (2021: 435) addresses the relationship between law (making and practising) and the city is the built environment. While devoting less attention to buildings' utilitarian functions (e.g., a courthouse as the place where disputes are resolved), he emphasizes the symbolic dimension, the meanings people associate with the buildings of law (courtrooms are related to authority or justice, for example). For Litwin, the built space serves as a "material repository" of international laws and its lawyers' history and presence; it communicates their practices, habits, ideals and beliefs. In this sense, the material infrastructure functions as an identity builder, as the instigator of community – it is in symbolically charged buildings and rooms that "the international lawyer enters the home of the invisible college of international lawyers". But of course, such edifices are progenitors of community not only in the symbolic sense, but also in very practical terms, as places of actual encounters and exchanges as at court hearings.

A second avenue Litwin (2021: 437f.; emphasis added) proposes investigating is the relationship between law (again, its making and practising) and cities' social and material contexts as frameworks for the shaping of legal practice and thinking. Attention should be drawn to the "urban context of social interactions within communities of international lawyers . . . [to] the clustering and directness of these urban interactions, and [to] the way the local frames that arise from these interactions and routines, and the meanings and shared understandings they create, may shape practices and affect the circulation of knowledge" (Litwin 2021: 437). For example, how "good" a legal argument is, and whether it becomes authoritative, may depend not only (or not even primarily) on its content, but whether it is

> finding acceptance in *local urban* embedded communities of practice formed around shared everyday urban socialization, routines and ways of doing things. . . . Put differently, the urban

might produce its own geographically bound epistemic culture, which frames international lawyers, and then naturalizes this situated point of view of the world. Naturalized since, from the situation of dense urban agglomerations and their long-distance networks with other similarly dense urban agglomerations, everything that is in-between is easier to overlook. In the process, the non-urban becomes something abstract and thus more readily subject to manipulation and exploitation. (Litwin 2021: 438)

Interestingly, Litwin expands the concept of "local urban embedded communities of practice" to what in urban studies is called the world city network. With the development of the investor-state dispute settlement apparatus, lawyers increasingly navigate the business districts of various global cities, while having regular meetings at the United Nations headquarters in New York City or the World Bank in Washington, DC. So, contrary to the attempts to portray contemporary international law as being "universal", it must be stated that it is not. It is shaped in global cities, and because these exist only as a cross-border network, it is also transnational.

Litwin is talking about international law, whereas my interest here is in attorneys specialized in labour and in patent law. There are certainly differences between them – the latter two, for example, do not have such symbolic and widely known buildings as the Peace Palace in The Hague, which houses the International Court of Justice. However, the built environment is not less important for labour and patent attorneys, even if the weighting between the "primary" (utilitarian) and "secondary" (symbolic) functions may shift. Even less can it be deduced that Litwin's basic thesis of "[i]nternational law is what cities do and how they think" should not also apply to other areas of law, too. Because labour and patent law may have a more direct impact on uneven development than international law, Litwin's claims about the practical – and that means political – significance of urban-biased lawmaking (and, in fact, global city-biased lawmaking) carries even more weight. For example, when he talks about "the non-urban becoming something abstract and thus more readily subject to manipulation and exploitation" because lawyers adopt a city-centred perspective, one might ask how much more this political influence must count when it comes to business services and the "plutocratic" milieu in global cities where they are developed and sold.

Interviews I conducted with patent attorneys, labour lawyers and lawyers in other business-related fields in Germany's global cities support Litwin's notion of the city as a decisive social and material milieu for the kinds of surplus transfer they facilitate or enact. Although I do not claim to be presenting the results of full-fledged research here, the empirical material does

119

confirm that being in the city is for lawyers a prerequisite for successfully practicing their profession, i.e., for helping their clients to maximize their profit. The density and diversity of an urban agglomeration is a frequently mentioned topic, both in terms of spatial proximity to clients, which is often – but not always – important, and to other knowledge-intensive business service firms.[35] As for the first aspect, it is, according to the interviewees, common that clients want to see their lawyer immediately. In such cases, it is helpful if the lawyer can say (s)he will stop by in 30 minutes. Whether this urgency is actually objectively justifiable in a specific case or whether it rather serves to create the fiction of constant availability and perfect service is of secondary importance, at least as long as law firms can turn this fiction into money. As to the second aspect, the density and diversity of a city (even if it is only a secondary global city such as Hamburg) implies a competitive advantage, because, as an interviewee confirms,

> there is, of course, more exchanges between the law firms. People know each other, of course they talk. And of course you notice market trends more when you are close to them than when you are far away. . . . You have a different network [here] in which you move more easily than if you were sitting somewhere else. . . . You look at what the others are doing and see if you can pick up on trends. And of course that's much easier when you're directly involved.

The city, or, to be precise, certain locations within it, offers further – albeit "only" soft – advantages for law firms. One refers to urban amenities. Highly paid lawyers want (and can demand from their firms) to be in places where they have a choice of expensive stores and restaurants around the corner. Symbolic capital in form of a good (i.e., prestigious) address is another critical aspect. Asked why they have their offices in expensive downtown locations and not on the outskirts, when potentially everything can be done with video conferencing, one lawyer replies that it is "part of our self-image, that we are not in a service centre in a cheap environment, but sit where people like to come". Another interviewee laughs: "We have frequently asked that ourselves. . . . [But] clients do not want this, well, clients want that their

---

35. Interviews were conducted before the outbreak of Covid-19, when video conferencing and the like were already practiced by the lawyers, but by no means as commonplace as they are today. Interviews were conducted in German and translated by the author.

lawyers are for free but they should be in representative locations, well, nobody wants to say: Well, my lawyer is in Pinneberg[36] . . . Let's put it like this: Pinneberg gives rise to doubts on the quality".

Especially for Berlin-based lawyers, physical proximity to decision-makers (members of parliament, ministers) and, perhaps more importantly, those who prepare decisions (ministerial bureaucracies), offers another agglomeration advantage, especially with regard to lobbying. If you seek to "somehow support certain legislative developments that are positive for the client", as one patent attorney put it, then "this is the perfect location here, Berlin . . . That's just the short distances, you see each other".

As to the advantages that knowledge-intensive business service providers derive from operating in a worldwide network of global cities, interviewees support the recurrent notion in the literature that easy access to knowledge at other locations – other jurisdictions, other political regulations, other firm cultures – is a decisive element for dealing with clients' requirements more quickly, more consistently and with higher quality outcomes. The partner from a global law firm in Hamburg claims that "our product is precisely that we can offer an internationally seamless service, services and accordingly . . . the product that we offer is in principle, quite often an internationally integrated advisory product, which we can offer better than other law firms that are only in the local market".

Finally, of the built environment, interviewees point to three kinds of infrastructure that are critical for their profession. They need meeting rooms in their office space to bring clients and lawyers together; they need suitable public transportation to be easily accessible for clients (proximity to the underground or rapid transit, with good connections to the airport); and they need – the most emphasized aspect – excellent IT infrastructure. Against this backdrop, the striking spatial differences in terms of infrastructural equipment (even in a country like Germany) underscore the importance of being located in global cities. Across Germany, only 60 per cent of business users have access to internet connection speeds of more than 1,000 Mbps, and only 16 per cent to fibre optic connections (FTTB/H, currently the state-of-the-art technology; data for 2022). Although communities where more than 90 per cent of users have access to the highest connection speeds account for less than 5 per cent of the area covered, all German global cities are amongst them. Importantly, the spatial differences in infrastructure are not only a matter of the urban–rural divide or of regional inequalities (such

---

36. Pinneberg, some 20 km northwest of Hamburg's CBD, is a 40,000-inhabitants town belonging to Hamburg's metropolitan region.

as the West–East disparities in Germany). Rather, it applies to cities, too, and even to the most important ones. Of the ten main industrial sites in Germany (all in former West Germany), only half have an access rate of more than 90 per cent. Stuttgart, for example, the centre of automotive and mechanical engineering production (with companies such as Mercedes-Benz, Porsche, Bosch, Siemens, Kodak and Lenovo) has an access rate of only 68 per cent; Leverkusen, an important centre for pharmaceutical industries, only 66 per cent (data source: BMDV & MIG 2022). In light of respondents' statements such as the one by a a patent lawyer in Berlin that "the most important thing is the technological equipment, especially IT", these cities have an obvious competitive disadvantage as a location for knowledge-intensive business services firms.

In sum, the interviews show that lawyers, whom I consider, due to the specialized knowledge they command, to be key agents in the production of uneven development, refer to the city – agglomeration, networks and the built environment – as a condition for working successfully. Accordingly, it is safe to say that van Heur's and Bassens' (2019: 591) notion that "elites depend on urban contexts for capital accumulation, consumption and leisure, and housing" applies to them. And I would add that capital accumulation is by far the most important aspect of the four mentioned. Economic elites might prefer certain cities for consumption or leisure reasons, but they *need* them for what Marx ([1890] 1962) called the *"Plusmacherei"*.

CITIFYING WORLD-SYSTEM ANALYSIS

To this point, the purpose of this chapter has been to suggest, by means of examples, what could be done empirically to scrutinize and thereby – hopefully – substantiate the idea of the Janus-facedness of cities. The selection of examples has been based, on the one hand, on different weapons of exploitation, but all of urban origin: buildings, predatory labour relations, the establishment of monopolies. The latter two I have dealt with in more detail and have also dealt with key actors: super-exploitation and corporate labour lawyers, the establishing of monopolies and lawyers specialized in intellectual property. Lawyers can therefore be called weapon-makers with good reason. These examples can be operationalized well, that is to say, they can be "translated" into concrete research (this also applies if one takes the built environment as a starting point). They could serve as a good starting point for a citified analysis of uneven development. Law offices offering global services that ultimately facilitate super-exploitation will be found in each of the aforementioned 500–600 cities that are the backbone of the world economy and that make up the world city network. One can start digging deeper wherever one wants – in the Global South or in the North, in key metropolises or at any peripheral node of Frank's (1969: 6) "chain of constellations of metropoles and satellites [which] relates all parts of the whole system from its metropolitan center in Europe or the United States to the farthest outpost in the Latin American countryside".

Fifty years after Immanuel Wallerstein published the founding manifesto and the first volume of his history of the modern world-system (Wallerstein 1974a, 1974b), such a project could help advance world-systems analysis by adding cities as a central category in the analysis of uneven development. As I have pointed out, Wallerstein claims that the capitalist world-system has "operated 'spatially'" (Hopkins & Wallerstein 1977: 112) since its emergence. The ability of its powerful actors to accumulate capital and concentrate it in their hands depended from the beginning on their use of geographical strategies, which at their core consisted in the creation of a unified economic arena – the global division of labour – and a fragmented political arena – the inter-state system. Accordingly, in world-systems analysis the geographical forms of "networks" (or commodity chains) and "territories" are treated as conceptual foundations of capitalism, while cities are treated only as a consequence of its expansion (and as concrete locations). Indeed, there are passages that would offer the potential for a deeper, urban theoretical-inspired engagement with uneven development, but this potential is not being exploited (or not recognized). Wallerstein notes, for example, that "the weakness of the towns" in Eastern Europe and "the comparative strength of the towns" in northwestern Europe in the sixteenth century were "beginning point[s]" for the incipient socio-spatial polarization in the world-system (Wallerstein 1974b: 97, 104). And he observes that what merchants needed to establish unequal exchange relations across extensive spaces in the sixteenth century, when both Eastern Europe and parts of North, Central and South America were incorporated into the world-system as peripheries, they learnt in their home cities: "In many ways the techniques of commercial gain used in the sixteenth century were merely an extension of the methods the towns learned to use *vis-à-vis* their immediate hinterland in the late Middle Ages" (*ibid.*: 119). But none of these passages are treated with analytical rigour. For Wallerstein the city is, Peter Taylor says (2018), an "outcome of a process rather than a process itself". Cities are treated as "core-making" places only in a descriptive way: cities cluster core economic activities, i.e. those that yield high profits and pay relatively well. They are, however, not treated as "core-making" in an analytical sense, or, as Taylor says, not as "proactive nodes" (Taylor 2013: 219). Cities, accordingly, *become* centres, but they *do not form* them.

In the late 1970s and into the 1980s, it seemed as if the poor treatment of cities in world-systems analysis might change. The emerging "urban political economy" brought important advances in understanding the role of cities and their elites in uneven development (e.g. Portes & Walton 1976; Roberts 1978; Timberlake 1985). In addition, Chase-Dunn's more quantitative work (e.g. 1985) sought to relate the changing contours of a "system of world cities" to the expansive dynamics and boundaries of the capitalist world economy. Yet, in the 1990s, interest waned – Smith (2003: 114) describes this period as "a short history of a promising perspective". A city-related world-systems spirit re-emerged with the early works of global city research (Sassen 1988, 1991) that were guided by an economic-geographical perspective on global-ization processes and devised as a citified analysis of economic power in the world economy. However, the impetus of world-systems research was quickly lost here as well, displaced on the one hand by an increased focus on issues of urban geography and on the other hand by the (ultimately very successful) efforts to record the world city network quantitatively (for an overview, see Parnreiter 2013).

In the face of this ebb and flow of world-systems analysis scholars' interest in cities, Taylor (2003: 131) claimed some time ago that it really was high time "[to cast] cities into a starring role in a world-systems analysis". Ten years later, the same author argued that Wallerstein's (1974a: 401) two mechan-isms and geographies of exploitation (the "appropriation of the surplus-value by an owner from a laborer [and the] . . . appropriation of surplus of the whole world-economy by core areas") "intersect as 'channels of exploitation' in cities" (Taylor 2013: 56) – reason enough, in fact, for putting them centre stage in world-systems analysis. That, as I said, has not happened so far.

This book has taken up Taylor's concern and is another attempt to advance the development of a citified perspective on uneven development and to find answers to Roberts' (1986: 459) concern by figuring out "how cities and the classes within them achieve control over other regions". For a number of reasons, a very appropriate way to do this is to start from commodity chain analysis. First, most production and trade is conducted within such chains (about 70 per cent, according to the OECD [2023]), which means that they actually capture and represent the basic structure of the world economy well, including, of course, both the production of wealth and exploitation. Second, commodity chains encompass *per definitionem* both the spheres of produc-tion and circulation, thus bringing together the vertical (owner–labourer) and horizontal (core–periphery) dimensions of exploitation, the interplay which Wallerstein identified as the essence of capitalism. Third, commodity chain analyses is considered to be well suited for analysis of the diverse mechanisms of capitalist exploitation and the corresponding production of uneven development. While chain-like descriptions of the economy (such as the French *filière* concept) have existed for longer, in world-systems analysis they evolved from empirical observation into an analytical category: "What we can learn from commodity chain analysis about the process of capital accumulation . . . and what it tells us about the distribution of the total surplus-value created?" (Bair 2009: 8) became the guiding question. Finally, as real existing structures of the world economy, commodity chains are shaped by both elements of Wallerstein's bifurcated geography – the spaces of flows of the unified economic division of labour, with all its extensions and ramifications, and the spaces of territories of the differentiated political regulation, with the gradation of profits, remuneration, and rights organized by nation states.

If we accept the definition of commodity chains as "*network(s)* of labor and production processes whose end result is a finished commodity" (Hopkins & Wallerstein 1986: 159; emphasis added), then it becomes obvious where the place of cities is or should be: a network consists not only of connections, but also of their nodes, the places where the links converge. When talking about human-made networks, it is about more than just convergence. The connections between the nodes, namely the flows of goods and people, of money and knowledge, are fed, organized, controlled from there. Cities are the "logical" places for that, for two reasons: first, they are, quite banal, the places where production is carried out which then "flows" to other places; where inputs are brought together; centres of trade and finance (i.e., clusters of specific inputs); and consumer markets (after all, a third of the world's population lives in cities with more than 300,000 inhabitants). Second, cities are the "logical" places from where economic flows are organized. Due to their very specific social and physical environments, cities are privileged – and in many cases probably the only – places for the production of the organizational capacities for economic and political governance and dominance. Accordingly, Wallerstein's bifurcated geography must be further developed into a three-layered one, with cities as the third element.

CHAPTER 6

CONCLUDING REMARKS

I have written this book to intervene in current debates on urban theory and on the nature of cities. First and foremost, I wanted to counter the one-sided, developmentalist discourse on cities which prevails today with a more comprehensive analysis of the role of cities in capitalism, one that acknowledges that cities' genius is Janus-faced. Their extraordinary capacity to produce innovation and efficiency does not only help to create prosperity, but it also constitutes the ground on which the development of the weapons of oppression and exploitation that underlie capitalist accumulation is based. Cities not only make people richer, smarter, greener, healthier and happier (cf. Glaeser 2011), as most of today's research (and related policy advice) suggests; they also work as "suction pumps" (Timberlake 1987: 51) that rob millions of people of the fruits of their labour and plunge them into misery.

As part of my rebuttal to the "the city has triumphed" notion, I recalled the work of scholars of earlier decades (and even centuries) that reveals, more or less clearly but always recognizably, how the urban properties of agglomeration, inter-city networks, and the built environment have been pressed into service, in different times and in different regions, for the purposes of enriching the few at the expense of the many. The works of Adam Smith and Karl Marx, of John Merrington and Bryan Roberts, of Fernand Braudel and Alejandro Portes and others show that the city has been a medium for capitalist accumulation since the advent of capitalism. And that in all senses, the city drives growth and creates the means of exploitation that underlies it. Cities have been – and continue to be – proactive nodes in production networks, and, simultaneously and for the same reasons, also proactive nodes in the asymmetric relations of the capitalist division of labour. We are currently running the risk of losing such insights. The book is a warning against this danger. "Harnessing urbanization for growth and poverty alleviation" (World Bank 2009b) is misleading advice, in political terms, resulting from an incorrect, because one-sided, analysis of how cities work. Misery does not come from a lack of cities, so it cannot be overcome by urbanization per se (which is not to say that cities and their economies cannot be important in overcoming poverty). For all the merit she has for our understanding of cities, Jane Jacobs is terribly wrong on this point – poverty does have causes, at least if we refer to the last 500 years, to the history of the capitalist world-system. Exploitation is one, arguably the most important, of these causes, and urban researchers would be well advised to recognize that the dark side of cities' creativity is their involvement in the production of ever new "innovative solutions" to secure domination and exploitation.

Recognizing cities' proactivity in the asymmetric connectivities of the capitalist division of labour has yet another impact on the debates on cities' nature. My argument that cities are – and remain – an *explanans* of uneven development implies rejecting the core thesis of the planetary urbanism literature, namely that the city has "become obsolete as an analytical social science tool" (Brenner & Schmid 2011: 13). Instead, I follow Scott and Storper (2015: 7) in this regard, who "assert the status of the city as a concrete, localized, scalar articulation within the space economy as a whole", with the specificity of the urban depending on cities' "contrasting qualities". Importantly, the analytical focus on the city that I propose does not correspond to a "methodological cityism" (Angelo & Wachsmuth 2015). Whereas in methodological nationalism (from which the notion of a methodological cityism is derived) the scale "nation state" is privileged over others without thorough explanation, making the city an *explanans* for economic development and its unevenness is justified in detail in the currents on which this book is built upon. The accounts of urban theory by Scott and Storper, Jacobs, Taylor, Massey, Roberts and others may differ greatly, but they have in common that they argue persuasively that and why cities should be put centre stage in social and economic analysis. "Urbanism as a way of life" may have spread out and single features of cities may have become available in an increasing number of places, but what makes cities really extraordinary are "spatial *intensities* of social relations" (Massey 1999: 76; emphasis added). And these remain the domain of a limited number of places, where the environment is socially and physically dense enough, sufficiently diverse and complex, to generate new ways of thinking and living. Cities are therefore more than just one scalar dimension of capitalism and its uneven development; they remain a central analytical category for understanding it.

A final note on the current debates about the nature of cities and how to research it: when I say that cities remain an explanans of uneven development, it is because my reflections on the Janus-facedness of cities owe much to the inspiring analyses of their role in emerging capitalism in Europe, in its gradual globalization from the sixteenth to the twenty-first century, in colonialism and in the subsequent peripheral development in Latin America. In this way, this book corresponds to the call for "a more cosmopolitan engagement with experiences and scholarship elsewhere" (Robinson 2006: 3) of literatures summarized under the labels of "comparative urbanism" and "Southern urban theory". This concern is particularly appropriate where the issue is exploitation and uneven development, not least because there have been intense debates revolving around this topic that are in danger of being forgotten today. Whether from a modernization-theoretical or a Marxist perspective (as in Hoselitz or González Casanova, respectively), or in the form of a dense description, as in Braudel, studies of cities and inter-city networks in peripheralized regions in the Global South or in Eastern Europe did much to inform my argument.

A critical intervention in the current attempts at theorizing the urban has been the main aim of this book. However, mine is not just an academic concern. The deep economic and social shocks of the last few years – rapid global warming, the subprime crisis of 2007–08, the Covid-19 pandemic, and the thousands of deaths of migrants in the Mediterranean and on other routes, to name just four that stand out – are increasingly eating away at the faith that capitalism can bring prosperity for everyone – even in the Global North. For the time being, right-wing and ultra-right parties and movements are primarily benefiting from the uncertainty and the fear of losing in the increasingly fierce distribution battles. Countering this requires a radical analysis, in the sense of going to the roots. And that will not be possible without correcting our notion of cities. As long as we persist in celebrating them, in seeing cities only as centres of promising innovation and as engines of economic growth, and turn a blind eye to how their creative potential is used to subjugate people in regions near and far, we are doomed to misspecify solutions to the big problems. Something we cannot really afford to do any longer.

REFERENCES

Allen, J. 2003. *Lost Geographies of Power*. Oxford: Blackwell.

Alonso, W. 1973. "Urban zero population growth". *Daedalus* 102(4): 191–206.

Amin, S. 1976. *Unequal Development: An Essay on the Social Formations of Peripheral Capitalism*. Brighton: Harvester Press.

Anderson, P. 1978. *Passages from Antiquity to Feudalism*. London: Verso.

Andrews, M. & A. Whalley 2022. "150 years of the geography of innovation". *Regional Science and Urban Economics* 94 (May): 1–8. https://doi.org/10.1016/j. regsciurbeco.2020.103627.

Angelo, H. & D. Wachsmuth 2015. "Urbanizing political ecology: a critique of methodological cityism". *International Journal of Urban and Regional Research* 39(1): 16–27. https://doi.org/10.1111/1468-2427.12105.

Arrighi, G. 1994. *The Long Twentieth Century: Money, Power, and the Origins of Our Times*. London: Verso.

Aust, H. & J. Nijman 2021. "The emerging roles of cities in international law: introductory remarks on practice, scholarship and the Handbook". In H. Aust, J. Nijman & M. Marcenko (eds), *Research Handbook on International Law and Cities*, 1–16. Cheltenham: Edward Elgar.

Bair, J. 2009. "Global commodity chains: genealogy and review". In J. Bair (ed.): *Frontiers of Commodity Chain Research*, 1–34. Stanford, CA: Stanford University Press.

Baran, P. 1973 [1957]. *The Political Economy of Growth*. New York: Monthly Review Press.

Baran, P. & P. Sweezy 1966. *Monopoly Capital: An Essay on the American Economic and Social Order*. New York: Monthly Review Press.

Bassens, D. *et al.* 2021. "Unpacking the advanced producer services complex in world cities: charting professional networks, localisation economies and markets". *Urban Studies* 58(4): 1286–302. https://doi.org/10.1177/0042098020908715.

Bathelt, H., A. Malmberg & P. Maskell 2004. "Clusters and knowledge: local buzz, global pipelines and the process of knowledge creation". *Progress in Human Geography* 28(1): 31–56. https://doi:10.1191/0309132504ph469oa.

Belina, B. 2013. *Raum. Zu den Grundlagen eines historisch-geographischen Materialismus.* Münster: Westfälisches Dampfboot.

Bensusán Areous, G. & K. Middlebrook 2012. *Organized Labor and Politics in Mexico: Changes, Continuities and Contradictions.* London: University of London Press.

Berlant, L. 2011. *Cruel Optimism.* Durham, NC: Duke University Press.

Berry, B. 1964. "Cities as systems within systems of cities". *Papers of the Regional Science Association* 13(1): 146–63. https://doi.org/10.1007/BF01942566.

Bettencourt, L., M. José Lobo & D. Strumsky 2007. "Invention in the city: increasing returns to patenting as a scaling function of metropolitan size". *Research Policy* 36: 107–20. https://doi:10.1016/j.respol.2006.09.026.

Bhaskar, R. 2005 [1979]. *The Possibility of Naturalism: A Philosophical Critique of the Contemporary Human Sciences.* Brighton: Harvester Press.

Boschma, R. 2005. "Proximity and innovation: a critical assessment". *Regional Studies* 39(1): 61–74. https://doi.org/10.1080/0034340052000320887.

Braudel, F. 1972. *The Mediterranean and the Mediterranean World in the Age of Philip II.* Volume I. New York: Harper & Row.

Braudel, F. 1977. *Afterthoughts on Material Civilization and Capitalism.* Baltimore, MD: John Hopkins University Press.

Braudel, F. 1983. *The Wheels of Commerce: Civilization and Capitalism 15th–18th Century.* Volume II. Berkeley, CA: University of California Press.

Braudel, F. 1984. *The Perspective of the World: Civilization and Capitalism 15th–18th Century.* Volume III. Glasgow: Collins.

Braudel, F. 1985. *The Structures of Everyday Life: Civilization and Capitalism: 15th–18th Century.* Volume I. Glasgow: Collins.

Braverman, I. *et al.* (eds) 2014. *The Expanding Spaces of Law: A Timely Legal Geography.* Stanford, CA: Stanford University Press.

Brechin, G. 2006. *Imperial San Francisco: Urban Power, Earthly Ruin.* Berkeley, CA: University of California Press.

Brenner, N. & C. Schmid 2011. "Planetary urbanisation". In M. Gandy (ed.): *Urban Constellations,* 10–13. Berlin: Jovis.

Brockerhoff, M. & E. Brennan 1998. "The poverty of cities in developing regions". *Population and Development Review* 24(1): 75–114. https://doi.org/10.2307/2808123.

Bundesamtes für Logitik und Mobilität 2023. Mautstatistiken Jahrestabellenwerk 2022. https://www.balm.bund.de/DE/Themen/Lkw-Maut/Mautstatistik/mautstatistik_node.html.

Bundesministerium für Digitales und Verkehr (BMDV) und Mobilfunkinfrastrukturgesellschaft mbH (MIG) 2022. Der Breitbandatlas.

https://www.bundesnetzagentur.de/DE/Fachthemen/Telekommunikation/ Breitband/breitbandatlas/start.html.

Callejas, D. 2021. General Motors Silao: Ven avance en sindicalismo. El T-MEC sienta las bases para mejorar derechos laborales. *Heraldo de México.* https://heraldodemexico.com.mx/economia/2021/8/19/general-motors-silao-ven-avance-en-sindicalismo-327376.html.

Camagni, R. & C. Salone 1993. "Network urban structures in northern Italy: elements for a theoretical framework". *Urban Studies* 30(6): 1053–64. https://doi.org/10.1080/00420989320080941.

Campling, L. *et al.* 2016. "Class dynamics of development: a methodological note". *Third World Quarterly* 37(10): 1745–67. https://doi:10.1080/01436597.2016. 1200440.

Castells, M. 1977. *The Urban Question: A Marxist Approach.* London: Edward Arnold.

Castells, M. 1983. "Crisis, planning, and the quality of life: managing the new historical relationships between space and society". *Environment and Planning D: Society and Space* 1(1): 3–21. https://doi:10.1068/d010003.

Chancel, L. *et al.* 2022. *World Inequality Report 2022.* World Inequality Lab.

Chase-Dunn, C. 1985. "The system of world cities, 800A.D.–1975. In M. Timberlake (ed.), *Urbanization in the World-Economy*, 269–92. Orlando, FL: Academic Press.

Cope, Z. 2019. *The Wealth of (Some) Nations: Imperialism and the Mechanics of Value Transfer.* London: Pluto.

Cronon, W. 1991. *Nature's Metropolis: Chicago and the Great West.* New York: Norton.

Davis, M. 2006. *Planet of Slums.* London: Verso.

Digitales Wörterbuch der deutschen Sprache (DWDS) 2022. "verstädtischung, verstadtlichung". Berlin-Brandenburgischen Akademie der Wissenschaften. https://www.dwds.de.

Dobbs, R. *et al.* 2011. *Urban World: Mapping the Economic Power of Cities.* McKinsey Global Institute.

Dunford, M. & D. Perrons 1983. *The Arena of Capital.* Basingstoke: Macmillan Education.

Duranton, G. & D. Puga 2004. "Micro-foundations of urban agglomeration economies". In J. Henderson & J.-F. Thisse (eds), *Handbook of Regional and Urban Economics Volume 4*, 2063–117. Amsterdam: Elsevier Science.

Emmanuel, A. 1972. *Unequal Exchange: A Study of the Imperialism of Trade.* New York: Monthly Review Press.

Euromonitor International 2019. *Passport: Cities Reports 2018.* London: Euromonitor Europe.

Fanon, F. 2005 [1961]. *The Wretched of the Earth.* New York: Grove Press.

Fitjar, R. & A. Rodríguez-Pose 2017. "Nothing is in the air". *Growth and Change* 48(1): 22–39. https://doi.org/10.1111/grow.12161.

Florida, R., P. Adler & C. Mellander 2017. "The city as innovation machine". *Regional Studies* 51(1): 86–96. https://doi.org/10.1080/00343404.2016.1255324.

Frank, A. 1967. *Capitalism and Underdevelopment in Latin America: Historical Studies of Chile and Brazil*. New York: Monthly Review Press.

Frank, A. 1969. *Latin America: Underdevelopment or Revolution: Essays on the Development of Underdevelopment and the Immediate Enemy*. New York: Monthly Review Press.

Friedmann, J. 1967. *Urban and Regional Development Advisory Program in Chile*. Santiago de Chile: Ford Foundation, Urban and Regional Advisory Program in Chile.

Friedmann, J. 1973. "The spatial organization of power in the development of urban systems". *Development and Change* 4(3): 12–50. https://doi.org/10.1111/j.1467-7660.1973.tb00643.x.

Gilbert, A. 1992. "Urban agglomeration and regional disparities". In A. Gilbert & J. Gugler (eds), *Cities, Poverty and Development: Urbanization in the Third World*, 33–61. Oxford: Oxford University Press.

Glaeser, E. 2011. *Triumph of the City: How Our Greatest Invention Makes Us Richer, Smarter, Greener, Healthier, and Happier*. London: Penguin.

González Casanova, P. 1965. "Internal colonialism and national development". *Studies in Comparative International Development* 1(4): 27–37. https://doi.org/10.1007/BF02800542.

Hadjimichalis, C. 1984. "The geographical transfer of value: notes on the spatiality of capitalism". *Environment and Planning D: Society and Space* 2(3): 329–45. https://doi.org/10.1068/d020329.

Hamann, B. 2010. *Hitler's Vienna: A Portrait of the Tyrant as a Young Man*. London: Tauris Parke.

Harvey, D. 1973. *Social Justice and the City*. Baltimore, MD: Johns Hopkins University Press.

Harvey, D. 1985. *The Urbanization of Capital*. Oxford: Blackwell.

Harvey, D. 2006 [1982]. *The Limits to Capital*. London: Verso.

Harvey, D. 2013. *A Companion to Marx's Capital*, Volume 2. London: Verso.

Hauser, P. 1961. *Urbanization in Latin America*. New York: International Documents Service.

Hibbert, A. 1965. "The economic policies of towns". In M. Postan, E. Rich & E. Miller (eds), *The Cambridge Economic History of Europe from the Decline of the Roman Empire. Volume III: Economic Organization and Policies in The Middle Ages*, 157–229. Cambridge: Cambridge University Press.

Hopkins, T. & I. Wallerstein 1977. "Patterns of development of the modern world-system". *Review: A Journal of the Fernand Braudel Center for the Study of Economies, Historical Systems and Civilizations* 1(2): 111–45.

Hopkins, T. & I. Wallerstein 1986. "Commodity chains in the world-economy prior to

1800". *Review: A Journal of the Fernand Braudel Center for the Study of Economies, Historical Systems and Civilizations* 10(1): 157–70.

Hoselitz, B. 1955. "Generative and parasitic cities". *Economic Development and Cultural Change* 3(3): 278–94.

Hyde, C. 1996. "Assembly-line architecture: Albert Kahn and the evolution of the US auto factory, 1905–1940". *Journal of the Society for Industrial Archeology* 22(2): 5–24.

International Labour Organization (ILO), Walk Free, and International Organization for Migration (IOM) 2022. *Global Estimates of Modern Slavery: Forced Labour and Forced Marriage*. Geneva: ILO.

International Trade Union Confederation (ITUC) 2022. "Multiple areas of crisis see workers' rights crumble: 2022 ITUC Global Rights Index". https://www.ituc-csi.org/2022-global-rights-index-en?lang=en.

Jacobs, J. 1961. *The Death and Life of Great American Cities*. New York: Vintage.

Jacobs, J. 1970. *The Economy of Cities*. New York: Random House.

Jacobs, J. 1985. *Cities and the Wealth of Nations: Principles of Economic Life*. New York: Vintage.

Jacobs, J. 1997. "Still challenging the way we think about cities". Interview by Steve Proffitt. *Los Angeles Times*, 12 October.

Kandell, J. 1990. *La Capital: The Biography of Mexico City*. New York: Henry Holt.

Katznelson, I. 1994. *Marxism and the City*. Oxford: Oxford University Press.

Kirby, A. 2012. "Current research on cities and its contribution to urban studies". *Cities* 29(1): 3–8. https://doi.org/10.1016/j.cities.2011.12.004.

Kluwer Law International 2021. "Top European patent prosecution firms of 2020". Kluwer Patent Blog. Last modified 22 July. http://patentblog.kluweriplaw.com/2021/07/22/top-european-patent-prosecution-firms-of-2020/.

Kostof, S. 1991. *The City Shaped: Urban Patterns and Meanings Through History*. New York: Bulfinch Press.

Lall, S. *et al.* 2021. *Pancakes to Pyramids: City Form to Promote Sustainable Growth*. Washington, DC: World Bank.

Lefebvre, H. 1991 [1974]. *The Production of Space*. Oxford: Blackwell.

Lefebvre, H. 2003 [1970]. *The Urban Revolution*. Minneapolis, MN: University of Minnesota Press.

Lipton, M. 1977. *Why Poor People Stay Poor: A Study of Urban Bias in World Development*. London: Temple Smith.

Litwin, D. 2021. "International lawyers and the city". In H. Aust, J. Nijman & M. Marcenko (eds), *Research Handbook on International Law and Cities*, 430–41. Cheltenham: Edward Elgar.

Logan, J. 2020. "The U.S. union avoidance industry goes global". *New Labor Forum* 29(1): 76–81. https://doi.org/10.1177/1095796019893336.

Maddison Project Database 2020. https://www.rug.nl/ggdc/historicaldevelopment/maddison/releases/maddison-project-database-2020.

Marini, R. 1973. *Dialéctica de Dependencia*. México DF: Ediciones Era, Serie Popular.

Marshall, A. 1920 [1890]. *Principles of Economics*. London: Macmillan.

Marx, K. 1960 [1869]. *Der achtzehnte Brumaire des Louis Bonaparte*. Berlin: Dietz Verlag.

Marx, K. 1962 [1890]. *Das Kapital. Kritik der politischen Ökonomie*. Erster Band. Berlin: Dietz Verlag.

Marx, K. 1973 [1857–61]. *Grundrisse: Foundations of the Critique of Political Economy (Rough Draft)*. Translated with a Foreword by M. Nicolaus. New York: Penguin.

Marx, K. 1976 [1890]. *Capital: A Critique of Political Economy*. Volume 1. New York: Penguin.

Marx, K. 1983 [1939]. *Grundrisse der Kritik der politischen Ökonomie*. Berlin: Dietz Verlag.

Marx, K. 1991 [1894]. *Capital: A Critique of Political Economy*. Volume 3. New York: Penguin.

Marx, K. & F. Engels 1955 [1890]. *The Communist Manifesto*. New York: Appleton-Century-Crofts.

Marx, K. & F. Engels 1974 [1845–46]. *The German Ideology*. Part One with selections from Parts Two and Three, together with Marx's Introduction to *A Critique of Political Economy*. London: Lawrence & Wishart.

Marx, K. & F. Engels 1978 [1845–46]. *Die deutsche Ideologie. Kritik der neuesten deutschen Philosophie in ihren Repräsentanten Feuerbach, B. Bauer und Stirner, und des deutschen Sozialismus in seinen verschiedenen Propheten (geschrieben 1845–1846, nach den Handschriften)*. Berlin: Dietz Verlag.

Massey, D. 1984. "Introduction: geography matters". In D. Massey & J. Allen (eds), *Geography Matters! A Reader*, 1–12. Cambridge: Cambridge University Press.

Massey, D. 1995 [1984]. *Spatial Divisions of Labour*. London: Macmillan.

Massey, D. 1999. *Power Geometrics and the Politics of Space-Time*. Heidelberg: University of Heidelberg.

Massey, D. 2004. "Uneven development: social change and spatial divisions of labour". In T. Barnes *et al.* (eds), *Reading Economic Geography*, 111–24. Oxford: Blackwell.

Massey, D. 2005. *For Space*. London: Sage.

Massey, D., J. Allen & S. Pile 1999. "Introduction". In D. Massey, J. Allen & S. Pile (eds), *City Worlds*, 1–2. London: Routledge.

McFarlane, C. 2011. "The city as a machine for learning". *Transactions of the Institute of British Geographers* 36(3): 360–76.

Merrington, J. 1975. "Town and country in the transition to capitalism". *New Left Review* 1(93): 1–22.

Moatsos, M. 2021. "Global extreme poverty: present and past since 1820". In OECD,

Global Extreme Poverty: Present and Past Since 1820. How Was Life? New Perspectives on Well-being and Global Inequality since 1820. Volume II. Paris: OECD Publishing.

Moore, J. 2010a. "'Amsterdam is standing on Norway': Part I: the alchemy of capital, empire and nature in the diaspora of silver, 1545–1648". *Journal of Agrarian Change* 10(1): 33–68.

Moore, J. 2010b. "'Amsterdam is standing on Norway': Part II: the global North Atlantic in the ecological revolution of the long seventeenth century". *Journal of Agrarian Change* 10(2): 188–227.

Morse, R. 1962. "Latin American cities: aspects of function and structure". *Comparative Studies in Society and History* 4(4): 473–93. https://doi.org/10.1017/S0010417500001420.

Morse, R. 1971. "Trends and issues in Latin American urban research, 1965–1970". *Latin American Research Review* 6(1): 3–52. https://doi.org/10.1017/S0023879100040796.

Mould, O. 2016. "Limitless urban theory? A response to Scott and Storper's, The Nature of Cities: The Scope and Limits of Urban Theory". *International Journal of Urban and Regional Research* 40(1): 157–63. https://doi.org/10.1111/1468-2427.12288.

Mumford, L. 1970 [1938]. *The Culture of Cities*. Orlando, FL: Harcourt Brace Joranovich.

OECD 2018. *OECD Regions and Cities at a Glance 2018*. Paris: OECD Publishing. https://doi.org/10.1787/reg_cit_glance-2018-en.

OECD 2022. "Employee compensation by activity". *Earnings and Wages*. https://doi.org/10.1787/7af78603-en.

OECD 2023. "Global value chains and trade". https://www.oecd.org/trade/topics/global-value-chains-and-trade/.

Parnreiter, C. 2013. "The global city tradition". In M. Acuto & W. Steele (eds), *Global City Challenges: Debating a Concept, Improving the Practice*, 15–32. Basingstoke: Palgrave Macmillan.

Parnreiter, C. 2019. "Global cities and the geographical transfer of value". *Urban Studies* 56(1): 81–96. https://doi.org/10.1177/0042098017722739.

Parnreiter, C. 2022. "The Janus-faced genius of cities". *Urban Studies* 59(7): 1315–33. https://doi.org/10.1177/00420980211007718.

Peck, J. 2017. "Uneven regional development". In D. Richardson *et al.* (eds), *The International Encyclopedia of Geography*, 7270–82. Hoboken, NJ: Wiley-Blackwell.

Phelps, N., M. Atienza & M. Arias 2018. "An invitation to the dark side of economic geography". *Environment and Planning A: Economy and Space* 50(1): 236–44. https://doi.org/10.1177/0308518X17739007.

Piketty, T. 2014. *Capital in the Twenty-First Century*. Cambridge, MA: Harvard University Press.

Portes, A. & J. Walton 1976. *Urban Latin America: The Political Condition from Above and Below*. Austin, TX: University of Texas Press.

Portes, A. 1977. "Urban Latin America: the political condition from above and below". In J. Abu-Lughod (ed.), *Third World Urbanization*, 59–70. London: Methuen.

Prebisch, R. 1950. *The Economic Development of Latin America and Its Principal Problems*. New York: United Nations Department of Economic Affairs, Economic Commission for Latin America (ECLA).

Pred, A. 1977. *City-Systems in Advanced Economies*. London: Hutchinson.

Pühretmayer, H. 2013. "Kritischer Realismus. Eine Wissenschaftstheorie der Internationalen Politischen Ökonomie". In J. Wullweber, A. Graf & M. Behrens (eds), *Theorien der Internationalen Politischen Ökonomie*, 217–32. Wiesbaden: Springer.

Raffer, K. 1987. *Unequal Exchange and the Evolution of the World System*. Basingstoke: Palgrave Macmillan.

Ravallion, M. 2007. "Urban poverty". *Finance & Development* 44(3): 15–17.

Reith, R. 2014. "Arcana artis? Wissens- und Technologietransfer im frühneuzeitlichen Handwerk". *Ferrum: Nachrichten aus der Eisenbibliothek* 86(1): 25–34. http://doi.org/10.5169/seals-391848.

Reynolds, S. 1997. *Kingdoms and Communities In Western Europe, 900–1300*. Second edn. Oxford: Clarendon Press.

Ridley, M. 2010. "When ideas have sex". TedGlobal Oxford. https://www.ted.com/talks/matt_ridley_when_ideas_have_sex/transcript.

Roberts, A. 2017. *Is International Law International?* Oxford: Oxford University Press.

Roberts, B. 1978. *Cities of Peasants: The Political Economy of Urbanization in the Third World*. London: Edward Arnold.

Roberts, B. 1986. "Review of Timberlake, M., *Urbanization in the World-Economy*". *International Journal of Urban and Regional Research* 10(3): 458–9. https://doi.org/10.1111/j.1468-2427.1986.tb00024.x.

Robins, N. 2011. *Mercury, Mining, and Empire: The Human and Ecological Cost of Colonial Silver Mining in the Andes*. Bloomington, IN: Indiana University Press.

Robinson, J. 2006. *Ordinary Cities: Between Modernity and Development*. London: Routledge.

Roth, J. & J. Boyoli 2021. "Inversión extranjera y empleo en México, ¿se están volviendo más simples?" Expansion, Opinion, 16 June; https://expansion.mx/opinion/2021/06/15/inversion-extranjera-empleo-mexico-simples.

Sassen, S. 1988. *The Mobility of Labor and Capital: A Study in International Investment and Capital Flow*. Cambridge: Cambridge University Press.

Sassen, S. 1991. *The Global City: New York, London, Tokyo*. Princeton, NJ: Princeton University Press.

Sayer, A. 2010. *Method in Social Science*. Second edn. London: Routledge.

Scott, A. 2017. *The Constitution of the City: Economy, Society, and Urbanization in the Capitalist Era*. Basingstoke: Palgrave Macmillan.

Scott, A. & M. Storper 2015. "The nature of cities: the scope and limits of urban theory".

International Journal of Urban and Regional Research 39(1): 1–15. https://doi.org/10.1111/1468-2427.12134.

Selwyn, B. 2019. "Poverty chains and global capitalism". *Competition & Change* 23(1): 71–97. https://doi.org/10.1177/1024529418809067.

Sennett, R. 2002 [1977]. *The Fall of Public Man*. London: Penguin.

Shearmur, R. 2012. "Are cities the font of innovation? A critical review of the literature on cities and innovation". *Cities* 29: 9–18. http://dx.doi.org/10.1016/j.cities. 2012.06.008.

Sheppard, E. 2016. *Limits to Globalization: The Disruptive Geographies of Capitalist Development*. Oxford: Oxford University Press.

Singer, H. 1950. "The distribution of gains between investing and borrowing countries". *American Economic Review* 40(2): 473–85.

Smith, A. 1977 [1776]. *An Inquiry into the Nature and Causes of the Wealth of Nations*. Chicago, IL: University of Chicago Press.

Smith, D. 1996. *Third World Cities in Global Perspective: The Political Economy of Uneven Urbanization*. Boulder, CO: Westview.

Smith, D. 2003. "Rediscovering cities and urbanization in the 21st century world-system". In W. Dunaway (ed.), *Emerging Issues in the 21st Century World-System*, Volume II, 111–29. Westport: Praeger.

Smith, J. 2016. *Imperialism in the Twenty-First Century: Globalization, Super-Exploitation, and Capitalism's Final Crisis*. New York: Monthly Review Press.

Smith, N. 2008 [1984]. *Uneven Development: Nature, Capital and the Production of Space*. Athens, GA: University of Georgia Press.

Soja, E. 1980. "The socio-spatial dialectic". *Annals of the Association of American Geographers* 70(2): 207–25. https://doi.org/10.1111/j.1467-8306.1980.tb01308.x.

Soja, E. 1989. *Postmodern Geographies: The Reassertion of Space in Critical Social Theory*. London: Verso.

Stanley, K. & J. Smith 1992. "The Detroit story: the crucible of Fordism". In I. Wallerstein & J. Smith (eds), *Creating and Transforming Households: The Constraints of the World-Economy*, 33–62. Cambridge: Cambridge University Press.

Stavenhagen, R. 2013. *The Emergence of Indigenous Peoples*. Berlin: Springer.

Storper, M. 2010. "Why does a city grow? Specialisation, human capital or institutions?" *Urban Studies* 47(10): 2027–50. https://doi.org/10.1177/0042098009359957.

Storper, M. 2013. *Keys to the City: How Economics, Institutions, Social Interaction, and Politics Shape Development*. Princeton, NJ: Princeton University Press.

Storper, M. & A. Venables 2004. "Buzz: face-to-face contact and the urban economy". *Journal of Economic Geography* 4(4): 351–70. https://doi.org/10.1093/jnlecg/lbh027.

Storper, M. & A. Scott 2016. "Current debates in urban theory: a critical assessment". *Urban Studies* 53(6): 1114–36. http://dx.doi.org/10.1177/0042098016634002.

Sunkel, O. 1972. "Big business and 'dependencia': a Latin American view". *Foreign Affairs* 50(3): 517–31. https://doi.org/10.2307/20037926.

Suwandi, I. 2019. *Value Chains: The New Economic Imperialism*. New York: Monthly Review Press.

Taylor, P. 2003. "Recasting world-systems analysis: city networks for nation-states". In W. Dunaway (ed.), *Emerging Issues in the 21st Century World-System*, Volume II, 130–40. Westport: Praeger.

Taylor, P. 2004. *World City Network: A Global Urban Analysis*. London: Routledge.

Taylor, P. 2013. *Extraordinary Cities: Millennia of Moral Syndrome, World-Systems and City/State Relations*. Cheltenham: Edward Elgar.

Taylor, P. 2018. Personal communication with author.

Taylor, P. *et al.* 2010a. *Global Urban Analysis: A Survey of Cities in Globalization*. London: Earthscan.

Taylor, P., M. Hoyler & R. Verbruggen 2010b. "External urban relational process: introducing central flow theory to complement central place theory". *Urban Studies* 47(13): 2803–18. https://doi.org/10.1177/0042098010377367.

Timberlake, M. (ed). 1985. *Urbanization in the World-Economy*. Orlando, FL: Academic Press.

Timberlake, M. 1987. "World-system theory and the study of comparative urbanization". In M. Smith & J. Feagin (eds), *The Capitalist City: Global Restructuring and Community Politics*, 37–65. Oxford: Blackwell.

US Census Bureau 2022. US Goods Trade: Imports and Exports by Related-Parties, 2021. https://www.census.gov/foreign-trade/Press-Release/related_party/rp21.pdf.

van Heur, B. & D. Bassens 2019. "An urban studies approach to elites: nurturing conceptual rigor and methodological pluralism". *Urban Geography* 40(5): 591–603. https://doi.org/10.1080/02723638.2018.1541372.

van Meeteren, M. & D. Bassens 2016. "World cities and the uneven geographies of financialization: unveiling stratification and hierarchy in the world city archipelago". *International Journal of Urban and Regional Research* 40(1): 62–81. https://doi.org/10.1111/1468-2427.12344.

van Meeteren, M. & J. Kleibert 2022. "The global division of labour as enduring archipelago: thinking through the spatiality of 'globalisation in reverse'". *Cambridge Journal of Regions, Economy and Society* 15(2): 389–406.

van Tielhof, M. 2002. *The Mother of All Trades: The Baltic Grain Trade in Amsterdam from the Late 16th to the Early 19th Century*. Leiden: Brill.

Vecco, M. 2020. "Genius loci as a meta-concept". *Journal of Cultural Heritage* 41 (Jan–Feb): 225–31.

von Arnim, R. & J. Stiglitz (eds) 2022. *The Great Polarization: How Ideas, Power, and Policies Drive Inequality*. New York: Columbia University Press.

Walker, R. 2016. "Why cities? A response". *International Journal of Urban and Regional Research* 40(1): 164–80. https://doi.org/10.1111/1468-2427.12335.

Wallerstein, I. 1974a. "The rise and future demise of the world capitalist system: concepts for comparative analysis". *Comparative Studies in Society and History* 16(4): 387–415.

Wallerstein, I. 1974b. *The Modern World System: Capitalist Agriculture and the Origins of the European World-Economy in the Sixteenth Century*. New York: Academic Press.

Wallerstein, I. 1983. *Historical Capitalism*. London: Verso.

Wallerstein, I. 1991. *Unthinking Social Science*. Cambridge: Polity.

Wallerstein, I. 1999. *The End of the World as We Know It: Social Science for the Twenty-First Century*. Minneapolis, MN: University of Minnesota Press.

Weber, A. 1922 [1909]. Über den Standort der Industrien. *Erster Teil: Reine Theorie des Standorts*. Tübingen: J. C. B. Mohr.

Wirth, L. 1938. "Urbanism as a way of life". *American Journal of Sociology* 44(1): 1–24.

Wójcik, D. 2013. "The dark side of NY-LON: financial centres and the global financial crisis". *Urban Studies* 50(13): 2736–52. https://doi.org/10.1177/0042098012474513.

World Bank 2009a. *World Development Report 2009: Reshaping Economic Geography*. Washington, DC: World Bank.

World Bank 2009b. *Systems of Cities: Harnessing Urbanization for Growth and Poverty Alleviation*. Washington, DC: World Bank.

World Bank 2013. *The World Bank Annual Report 2013*. Washington, DC: World Bank.

World Bank 2021. "New World Bank report covering 10,000 cities shows shape of urban growth underpins livability and sustainable growth". Press release. https://www.worldbank.org/en/news/press-release/2021/06/01/new-world-bank-report-covering-10-000-cities-shows-shape-of-urban-growth-underpins-livability-and-sustainable-growth

World Bank 2022. "World Development Indicators". Databank. https://databank.worldbank.org/source/world-development-indicators# (accessed 09/09/2023).

World Bank Institute 2010. "Cities as engines of economic growth". YouTube. www.youtube.com/watch?v=mANzdLhxXXw.

World Intellectual Property Organization 2023. "Intellectual Property Statistics". https://www.wipo.int/ipstats/en/ (accessed 15/09/2023).

INDEX